"TEN LONG DAYS"

by

Joan De Souza

Grosvenor House
Publishing Limited

This book is published by
Grosvenor House Publishing Ltd
Link House
140 The Broadway, Tolworth, Surrey, KT6 7HT.
www.grosvenorhousepublishing.co.uk

A CIP record for this book
is available from the British Library

ISBN 978-1-78623-424-7

FOREWORD

This is essentially my story, as I remember it, with no verification sought from anyone. No diary notes survived so none were available for me to draw on.

Once I had begun I realised that I was unlocking a part of my memory which had recorded in unbelievable detail, a perilous episode in my life. The story unfolds with clarity although I had experienced this at such a young age and here I am recalling it so many years later. It seemed it was an experience which the years could not dim from my memory.

It is written as my personal Testimony to the Inspiration of my beloved Mother whose Faith and indomitable spirit were largely responsible for our survival. Her loving caring nature has been the Beacon of my life and we were to learn much from her example to strengthen our Faith in God and mankind.

However, I realise that with my limited degree of literary skill I could have sadly fallen short of giving the reader the benefit of absorbing the story as I wish it to be portrayed. Perhaps the nature of the Story will speak for itself. There have no doubt been other tragic accounts of this perilous Trek by those brave survivors like ourselves but as far as I am aware, we were the only family to embark on this particular route from Sumprabum through the mountainous region of the Kachin Hills. We endured this for three months and only met up with the main route of evacuees when we reached the Hukawng valley.

As this story's ending confirmed I owed so much to my beloved husband's help and encouragement during the writing of "Ten Long Days". He was so keen on me achieving publication and constantly encouraged me to return to having it published. He felt that it was a story that had to be told.

Sadly I failed to do this, mainly due to my desire to concentrate on maintaining our happy lives despite several serious medical battles which he survived through his courage and my loving support. I came very near to returning to achieve publication when I lost my beloved Gerry at the beginning of 2017 after 65 wonderful years together.

Although heart broken and far less able to fulfil his wish, I feel strongly that I owe it to his memory to do this now. It is with this heartfelt desire that I am now, after more than 50 years since I first embarked on writing my story, filled with the resolve to honour his wish.

CONTENTS

CHAPTER ONE

"Winning the War"

With the dropping of the first Japanese bombs on Rangoon in December 1941, our lives were to change in a way we could never have envisaged. Being the youngest member of a British family in pre-war Burma, enjoying the comforts and luxuries of a good home, I was ill prepared for the hardships that were to befall us within the ensuing months. This is my Story of that period of my life which has never been told till now and in recalling the events in detail I have had to relive the experience in my mind, heartbreaking though much of it was. I found it a relief to have set it out on paper for the benefit of our family and anyone else interested in this tragic and unforgettable experience.

My father was employed by The Burmah Oil Company at Syriam, near Rangoon, in Burma. It was here that I enjoyed a sheltered upbringing where, as a child, I had been protected from witnessing the passing of a funeral procession or the hearsay of domestic tragedies. My eleven year old world, for the most part, allowed for no possibility other than happy times in the care of a loving family. However, during the next few months my family and I were to embark on a Trek from Burma to India during which we were to witness sights which drove adults beyond the limits of sanity and experience situations which beggar description in their horror. Much of it reduced us to a physical and mental condition, where only our Faith gave us the hope we needed to carry us past the gates of a waiting death. Whilst the War in Europe had certainly captured our attention and concern, we were at this time under no threat to our hitherto secure, happy and peaceful lives.

My parents were naturally watchful of and interested in the progress of the War in Europe, my Father being kept fully informed by the London Gazette which was on regular order from London. One particular 'zone' of interest to me was the large Map my Father had pinned to one of the walls in his room. This he would update daily on receipt of news on the 'Wireless', as it was known in those days, by moving the respective Flags on the Map to indicate Nazi advances in Europe. It was now that the wretched Swastika first registered in my mind. I was always a very inquisitive child who was, more than any other member of my family, bearing in mind my age, interested in all that was going on in my world and the wider world too. I would always ask questions of my Father as to what the War in Europe could mean to us and how we were going to 'win the war'!! I remember my Father expressing concern at the rate at which Nazi Flags were being pinned to the Map of Eastern Europe and then France bringing them ever nearer to England. My sister Patsy who was a bright student herself was not unduly concerned, as it seemed were most of the rest of my family, with the exception of my Father.

CHAPTER TWO

"Our Home in Burma"

So it was that we carried on our daily lives in this beautiful Country of Burma, enjoying a lifestyle that would be the envy of many. Our home in Syriam, across the water from Rangoon, was to my mind a place of love and happiness, a warm welcome always being extended by my dear Mother, whose capacity for loving people and enjoying their company was boundless. Our Home was usually full not only because our family comprised 7 adults and two children (my sister Patsy and myself being the 'follow-up' family of two after a break of eight years) but also because our large dining table nearly always served an extra couple of guests. Visitors were invited to join us for meals and a happy exchange of chatter.

Pagoda in Rangoon

My dear Mother's interest in helping the poor and needy was very much part of our lives and particularly her devotion to helping with sick native children. I remember sitting by her side chatting to her and 'helping' as her sewing machine whirred on at some speed churning out small garments for those little ones. Very often she would take medicinal needs from our home when visiting them and I recall 'rolling' many bandages for her 'First Aid' box.

In 1940 my sister Patsy and myself had transferred to a new Catholic School in Syriam which we loved. It was only a small branch of the main Convent in Rangoon and we were privileged to be educated by highly qualified and able teachers, in very small classes, which meant near to private tuition. We were very happy here and also benefitted from starting to learn music with a Nun, who was both able and qualified from the London School of Music and again because of our small numbers, we were given so much individual attention. Such happy days enjoying so many activities whilst having great times as a family too.

As December 1941 arrived, we children were looking forward, as always, to Christmas and I remember Patsy and myself going to Rangoon by Launch, with my Mother, early in the month. This was always a source of great excitement to us and as "Father Christmas had stopped calling" we each chose our 'big present' i.e. a life size doll. One that could move and do things! I recall us returning home excited but promising to forget what we had done so that we keep the surprise of Christmas day intact! It was soon after this that my Brother Victor and Sister Joyce fell ill and I remember the word Para-Typhoid being spoken of constantly. They were both fairly ill - my Brother being treated at our local hospital.

At this very same time it seemed that the cracks in our world were appearing at a pace because news was abounding, concerning the very real threat of Japan declaring war on Great Britain, of which we were a part, as her Colony. It was on or about the 9th of December that we first heard the sound of sirens wailing warning us of enemy aircraft approaching. These were reconnaissance aircraft surveying their possible targets no doubt. Japan had declared war on Great Britain and we were soon to realise that the troops scheduled to hold on to Burma were far short of requirements. So many thousands of brave Men's lives were sacrificed in the attempt. Although we were not to know it at the time, history tells us that much political activity had transpired between the 'Burmese influential' and Japanese Military authorities prior to the war. This resulted in Britain not having the support of a large section of the Burmese political hierarchy and youth organisations in such a war. There was also much 5th Columnist activity going on in Burma at this time and these combined factors made the Japanese invasion of Burma all the easier for them.

We were now in the second week of December, and my Father had arranged for his 'workmen' to dig a trench in our garden, which he hoped would provide some form of shelter for us in the event of Japanese Air Raids. This was done in a great hurry because everyone knew that there was no time to lose if we hoped to survive.

Us children were somewhat excited at the prospect of sleeping in a trench lit by the 2 candles, which had been positioned deep within so as not to show any light at the entrance and exit, in case this was spotted by enemy aircraft!

The naivety of our age made us less aware of the frightening nature of our plight. It seemed that our lives were in full fall at this point because both Patsy and myself had contracted Typhoid and were confined to our beds with our Company Doctor in attendance. My Mother, as always, proved the perfect Nurse as well as having to keep our rocking ship afloat. It was here that my dear Maternal Grandmother's fear took hold and carried on till her death. She would be crying and shaking with fear, poor darling, each time we heard the siren and fled to the trench - night and day.

*My Grandmother with Patsy on her left
and me on her right behind her*

Whereas Patsy and myself would have normally been hugging and reassuring her, we were so ill at the time and having to be nursed under dreadful circumstances ourselves, so we could not comfort her in our special way. The other grown-ups did give her their loving support but there were so many needs to be covered at this awful time. So great was her fear that I remember her becoming hysterical when I could not stop my cat purring whilst we were in the Trench - she felt it might have broken the silence we needed to listen out for approaching air craft! My tears in remembering this so vividly is testimony to the special place she held in our hearts.

CHAPTER THREE

"Bombing of Rangoon"

Whilst we had experienced daily Air Raid Sirens which meant conveying us to and from the trench wrapped in blankets, carried by whoever was able, we had not yet experienced the terror of bombing. This was to change in the third week of December when Rangoon was badly bombed and, as we were not that far away, we felt the impact. It was during the raid on 23rd December 1941 that my brother Victor's girlfriend - Gloria's family were killed. I remember my brother who was still recovering from Typhoid and in a weak state, insisting on going to Rangoon to bring Gloria to us.

Christmas was, as never known before, with constant air threats and sirens sounding throughout the day, my Father being called to his post as were most Oil Company senior personnel. Patsy and myself were bedridden with a high fever and were unable to eat anything, my dear mother being our constant nurse. Glucose and a type of milky drink are all I remember us being given at the time. Christmas Lunch for the grown-ups was tinned ham, tinned peas and tinned potatoes. This was confirmed by my brother-in-law, George, who was at that time courting my eldest sister and who was very much part of our lives. Our servants had fled with the threat of bombing. Food stores remained closed. We were to depend on whatever was stored in our houses. Whilst raids on Rangoon continued, we in Syriam had so far escaped this but we were to soon realise that this was because Syriam was the Oil Refinery and the Japanese had planned to capture all the refined oil for their own military purposes.

By the second week in January, our Company Doctor having given his approval, my Parents decided that we could lose no time in leaving Syriam and heading for my Uncle Jim's home in Myitkyina, the northernmost town in Burma. My Uncle was working for the Government as a Senior Excise Superintendent and he was comfortably settled there at this time. It was felt that we would be safe here till arrangements could be made for us to be evacuated by Air to India. My father was to remain at Syriam with the Burmah Oil Company as part of the few personnel who were retained for the demolition of the Refinery at the appointed hour, thus depriving the Japanese of this much valued gain. They were then to have been evacuated by sea to India which, though ultimately successful, turned out to be a hazardous and dangerous escape for them.

The Japanese launched the land campaign, which the air attacks on Rangoon preceded, in the third week of January 1942. Whilst we were well aware of the speed at which the War was overtaking us, we nevertheless retained a prayerful hope that we would some day be able to return to our home. With me were my Mother, Grandmother, sisters Joyce, Phyllis and Patsy, brothers Victor and Frank and Victor's girlfriend Gloria who had been orphaned by the first Japanese raid on Rangoon.

My brothers Frank & Victor (rear) - Patsy, Joyce,
Phyllis & myself (1941)

We set out from Rangoon at the end of January with heavy
hearts at having to leave my Father behind, though he tried
to reassure us that, if demolition became necessary, the Oil
Company would ensure that they be evacuated to India by
Sea. Not many words were exchanged at this parting for our
hearts were heavy. I can remember when later we tried to
comfort my Mother by expressing our confidence that soon
we would be together again, she shook her head sadly as if
she knew that this was for her a final farewell.

My much loved Mother & Father

The journey up to Myitkyina by Rail took three days and for my sister Patsy and myself at least, being the younger members of the family; it was an adventure, for we were still blissfully ignorant of the seriousness of our plight. To us it was the fulfilment of a long cherished desire to travel up to my Uncle's home and to my dear Mother's credit, I must admit that whatever she felt at the time, she in no way curtailed our enjoyment of the long rail journey. The adult members of our family were well aware of the seriousness of our situation and the mood was sombre and fearful. However, my older brother Victor made sure that us younger ones were given the chance to enjoy the excitement of our adventure. We had insisted on bringing with us our newly acquired Dolls which were to remain with us for yet a while. I also took my Black Cat with us because I could not bear to leave him behind. "Blacky" was to travel with me to Sumprabum!

CHAPTER FOUR

"Arrival at Myitkyina"

We arrived in Myitkyina and were soon comfortably settled. First in my Uncle's home and then in a home on our own where we awaited developments. At this stage Myitkyina, in our minds, seemed safe but this was to soon change.

The Japanese army was advancing from the south, at a pace, increasing the flow of Refugees to bursting point. With the hope of evacuation by Air, thousands poured into Myitkyina night and day and very soon the problems from such an influx were prevalent. Although every available building of reasonable size was taken over as an Evacuee Centre, this little town was soon over-run with homeless families clutching their pitiful bundles of clothing and perhaps one or two personal treasures. By this time many families had become parted from each other in the chaos of fleeing to safety. There were many frightened people running around, almost aimlessly trying to get word of one or other member of their family, who had become 'lost' in the scramble to escape. God's help was being invoked by screaming individuals, so desperate to escape their dilemma.

Although we had been amongst the first families to register our names on the Evacuation Roll, it seemed that our destiny did not allow for this. At first, the plight of those who were homeless moved my Mother to give way to their more pressing need. In agreement with my Uncle, she felt sure that however serious the position was, we would be evacuated in good time. We were not to know that our hopes were to be thwarted by the sudden illness of my brother Frank, who was soon admitted to hospital with pneumonia.

It was now early April and the Japanese Army was advancing ever nearer. The need for evacuation became more pressing with each day and what little semblance of organisation which had at first been established, was rapidly diminishing, under pressure from the thousands who continued to pour in. Chaos ensued, as did the spread of disease in such unhygienic conditions. The town of Myitkyina was enveloped in confusion and general chaos with people running everywhere, pleading for help to be evacuated but by this time no effective Authority existed.

According to the Order of the Evacuation Roll which had at first been established, we had been promised seats on the next Aircraft in, but by this time, my Mother had been informed by medical authorities that my brother's condition was such that an air flight could prove fatal! I well remember the family discussion on this matter, my Mother preferring that the rest of us go ahead, leaving her with my brother to follow on. However, we were unanimous in our refusal to split the family in such a critical situation. So, in spite of my Mother's attempted persuasion, we had decided to remain together come what may. We did, of course, anticipate this merely being a delay of a few days before we would once again qualify for places on another plane.

In the days that followed my brother gradually improved but whereas he would normally have been hospitalised for longer, the situation was so critical that my Mother was compelled to bring him home, assuming full responsibility.

Part of the chaos in the Town seemed to have been redirected to the road going south, with some native families, in the face of starvation and sheer fatigue, resorting to re-entry into territory soon to be overrun by the Japanese army. Others were heading north for the hills to escape by a yet unknown and untested route - most of whom were to perish in the attempt.

Some Burmese families were seeking refuge in the small villages across the river from Myitkyina. However, there still remained hundreds of desperate people who, without any direction, ran around seeking 'help'. So many families had been split up in the general chaos, that the streets in the town were now like a maze with people trying to find their loved ones, calling their names amidst tears. At this stage we were still hopeful of being evacuated by Air but the speed at which developments were taking place caused my Mother and Uncle to reassess the situation in a hurry.

Things happened fast that evening. Our entire family, including my Father's brother Arthur, his wife and three children and another Aunt, and her two daughters who had joined us during the past month, were now all making our way to my Uncle Jim's home. For this move, which was made at night and in haste, we took with us a prepared bag of necessities and a few of our most prized possessions, which had been packed in the event of us being evacuated by Aircraft.

That night we children were given a hot drink and tucked into bed with what we felt was undue haste and we sensed the seriousness of the situation by the solemn looks on the adult faces around us. We lay there, unable to sleep, and I remember hearing gun fire which had an unnerving effect on the grown-ups, who kept looking in on us far more than was necessary, as if to reassure themselves.

CHAPTER FIVE

"Myitkyina under Siege"

During the past month or so, Japanese Reconnaissance planes had often flown over and we were used to hearing the wail of the siren, so hearing it again on this particular night did not trouble us unduly. The necessary precautions concerning lighting were observed, and so we eventually drifted into a troubled sleep in the light of shaded oil lanterns.

So tense was the situation that we had been put to bed fully dressed but without our shoes and when we were disturbed by the loud murmur of voices and general activity, amidst the light of these lamps, we realised that this was 'Zero hour'. Somehow, no one spoke much, other than receiving directions and following them as calmly as possible. We piled into the two Cars belonging to my Uncles, each clutching our little bags, further reduced in size of necessity. If we were to be fortunate enough to get on an Aircraft, it would be a case of going only as we stood.

It was the 5th of May 1942 and we were on our way to the Aerodrome in the half-light of dawn. I remember hearing the adult conversation focus on the report that two Dakotas were expected to touch down in the early hours and it seemed that my Uncle had been given the tip-off concerning this, hence our flight to the Airfield at this hour. However, when we arrived at the Airfield there were several other cars parked in the vicinity and each little group of people eyed the other with a mixture of sympathy and suspicion, each looking for a sign of hope to appear out of that beautiful dawn sky.

We had waited a long while without anything happening and with six children in the party, we were in need of some refreshment. We made for a building at the far end of the Airfield where we could take some of the refreshments we had brought with us and use the toilet facilities available. These were horrendously unhygienic by this time. We were of course to keep the landing strip in view in the event of any activity.

Within a few minutes of entering the small building we heard the loud drone of an Aircraft engine which told us that one was about to land. By the time we got out and made for the spot where it had landed, some little distance away, people had converged on it from every direction. It seemed that the vegetation bordering the Airfield was sheltering hundreds of desperate people waiting for a means of escape! The Pilot did of course have to limit the number acceptable and so it was that we and hundreds of others were turned away. It was understood that other Aircraft were to follow so, though anxious, we were not too disheartened. However, this time we were determined to stay where we were and not miss our chance of evacuation. We picked a spot by the runway itself at which we gathered as a group amongst the many other desperate souls who shared our forlorn hope.

There we waited and time seemed endless. Knowing that we were to remain where we were and not leave our chosen space come what may, made our natural needs more evident and urgent so we were suffering in all kinds of ways. Seconds were like minutes and minutes like hours during this agonising fearful wait. It seemed that the traumas of the previous day were being swallowed by the dawn which brought us to a far more threatening need. All our senses were now directed towards our escape by Air. The sky was being lightened by the rising Sun, its warmth beating down on us bedraggled - and frightened souls, bleary eyed from lack of sleep. The 'Rising Sun' was of course the emblem which brought fear to our hearts as it was the emblem of Japan, which identified the planes which were to bring death and destruction to us.

Several other families had arrived at the Airfield by now, and we stood there, small groups of very troubled people, talking quietly, barely taking our eyes off the horizon where, at that moment, all our hopes lay. Patsy and I held on to my Mother not daring to lose sight of her. Men from other groups joined us chiefly for reassurance from my Uncle who had taken such an active part in the evacuation and they in turn brought us reports of the Japanese Army being very near.

It was a big moment of decision for my Uncles who had already begun to fear the urgency imposed by such reports and there seemed no alternative but to move us out and head as far north as possible to consider our next move. Having decided this, we once again crammed ourselves into the two Cars and headed back towards my Uncle Jim's home where we planned to pick up supplies and above all, as much petrol as we could carry. At this stage it seemed that our only option was to make for the hills.

We had barely left the Airfield when the drone of aircraft engines filled the air and there, low on the horizon appeared two Dakotas' sweeping around to line up for a touchdown. At this, we immediately turned in our tracks, attempting to make it to the Airfield in time. As we came in sight of it, we were aghast to see one of the Aircraft already airborne, having taken on its full capacity of passengers in haste. Still we were hopeful as to our chances of getting on the second plane.

However our hopes were short lived for as we joined the road running parallel to the Airfield our attention was diverted from our goal to the two silver grey Aircraft, high on the horizon heading in our direction. The adults in our party sensed that these were no 'Friendly' or 'Reconnaissance' aircraft. I well remember the haste with which my Uncles stopped the Cars and urged us to run as fast as our terrified limbs could carry us to the shelter of a fragile bridge some thirty or so yards away.

There was no time to give much thought as to the contents of the ditch into which we had thrown ourselves. By now the Japanese fighters had borne down on the airfield strafing it with machine gun fire - returning time and time again, leaving in its wake many dead, wounded and a badly damaged aircraft. We remained thus - much muddied by our sheltering in the bog filled ditch, - with us younger ones crying - too frightened to move. After a long wait we were reassured by my Uncles and the older members of our family that the Japanese Aircraft had turned, making their way south. At this point my Uncle who knew there was no time to lose directed us to the cars and we again hurriedly made for my Uncle's home to decide our next move. For humanitarian reasons we wanted to return to the Airfield to see whether we could help those poor unfortunate people for we knew there would be many dead, dying and injured amongst them. However, my Uncle felt that with so many women and children in his care, his duty was to ensure our safety and this meant acting without delay.

We learned later that the Japanese aircraft returned again and again bombing the Airfield relentlessly making its use for further evacuation impossible. Sadly we were also to hear that a family who had taken refuge in my Uncle's home, late on the previous night, had been killed in these raids as were scores of other desperate people.

Unbelievably, a few years later in my life, I came to realise that my beloved Gerry was, with his family, amongst the scores of people who, like us, were fighting to escape by plane from the airstrip at Myitkyina. At the same point at which we decided to abort out initial attempt to escape by Air, his family chose to leave the Airstrip and make their way to a village south of Myitkyina, where they hoped to find shelter and survive persecution. Although they suffered many dangers and privations they did survive the occupation having lost his Father and Grandmother.

Gerry himself, at the age of 16, as the eldest male member of the family took on the full responsibility of their survival and at the near end of the war was himself imprisoned by the Japanese for stealing food for their pressing need off a passing train. It was only the timely intervention of Allied Forces bombing the Japanese Operational Control that freed the prisoners and so saved his life.

So it was that yet another very important part of my destiny was played out to secure my truly happy marriage and future.

As we passed through the Town we noticed that it was now eclipsed by an eerie silence - open doors swaying in the breeze. An unwholesome stench seemed to fill the air. I remember noticing the stillness which had taken over from the noisy confusion existing some hours previously. The Railway Station, which had buzzed with activity and whose siding sheds had provided shelter for so many cold and hungry humans, seemed strangely quiet. There were unmanned engines lying here and there. The overall picture was of impending doom as we passed through Myitkyina for the last time, driving as fast as we could in our overloaded cars towards my Uncle Jim's home. Shots were being fired all around us but we did not wait to see who was doing the firing.

We picked up whatever supplies we could carry at my Uncle's home and with much haste, set out for the village of Sumprabum - some hundred or so tortuous twisting miles to the North. We had been given information as to the possibility of sheltering here 'out of interested reach' by the Japanese forces!

CHAPTER SIX

"Destination Sumprabum"

On leaving Myitkyina we soon found ourselves en route to the Hills along a narrow road in company with thousands of footsore, hapless refugees, clutching their little bundles. There were broken down Cars, bicycles and even Bullock Carts littered along the path. Thousands of people were 'scrambling' to what they thought could be safety - totally ignorant of what lay ahead. The further we travelled the greater the number. My Uncles were forced to manoeuvre our Cars between all this chaos and suffering in order to take us to safety - as was hoped. My dear Mother as always was touched and saddened by the plight of these poor people but we had very soon come to realise that it was going to be a fight to survive. However, at this stage no one knew quite what we were hoping to reach! For the most part fear and ignorance kept us focusing on the 'Road Ahead'!

We kept going - staying in the Cars overnight on one occasion, scrambling for hidden places to cater for bodily needs! We managed to bed down in a Bungalow on one night and reached the 102-mile post the next day. (It was at this Bungalow that our Dolls were left behind together with a bag of clothing - tears were shed but soon brought into place amidst the danger we were in). Here we witnessed a huge gathering of desolate souls, scrambling around trying to find hope, shelter and food and my Uncles decided that we not stay here but proceed to Sumprabum.

We had brought with us a small supply of tinned food and were able to replenish our stock at Bungalows we passed en route, with whatever little was to be found in their store cupboard. Although troubled in mind we had not yet suffered the total lack of food and drink. The road being not much more than a Cart track in places and for the most part skirting steep hillsides, we were not able to cover any distance in a day. So it was that we took a few days to cover these 100 odd miles by car. This experience in itself was nerve shattering and I remember us often crying hysterically at the dangerous predicament we found ourselves in. Old overcrowded cars carrying us over tracks that barely afforded room for all four wheels to traverse safely. Hugging hillsides with deep ravines on the other!

We had been travelling for two days when we met two Army Personnel who informed us that there were reports of the Military supposedly organising groups of evacuees, who were to be given assistance and supplies for their Trek to India from the 102nd mile escape route. As we were still uncertain as to our plans, my Uncle felt it worth investigating this rumour and so we headed back to the 102nd mile point, which we had so recently passed. The fear we had endured in reaching the point we were at was to be repeated it seemed but, by now, every decision made was to have its perils. Balancing one danger against another was difficult enough but balancing this in circumstances of ignorance was even worse as we were to discover.

On returning to the 102nd mile point we were sickened and depressed at the misery surrounding us for by this time, many more thousands of desperate, frightened and tired people had headed here looking for some little hope that could be offered of reaching freedom safely. Mothers were clutching their children and crying. The troubled feelings of the men folk were reflected in their solemn faces. The rain beat down and people were crowding for the shelter of the only Bungalow which was nevertheless totally inadequate for the numbers there.

Little groups of people were rigging makeshift tents to try and keep dry under these monsoon conditions without success. For the first time we were to witness so many weeping women and children. Men were jostling for position in claiming a patch on which to settle. It seemed that all hope of survival was quickly disappearing into the muddy squalor surrounding them. My dear Mother, in spite of our own predicament was deeply moved by the sad plight of these poor people and she was soon reaching out to comfort and encourage them amidst her tears. This was to be our first real taste of what was to befall us later.

At this point my Brother Victor came upon two Army Officers whom we knew well and who had joined us for Meals at our table in Syriam during peacetime. Through them we managed to secure a small corner of a room in the Bungalow. Though we were by no means comfortable, we were at least sheltered from the rain and able to stem our hunger with dry biscuits and a tin of fruit. I remember falling asleep on my Mother's lap, whilst the decision which we had come to make was still being debated. It seemed that any hope expressed was based on unfounded information, as we were to later discover, when learning of the thousands of lives lost on this fateful route. Some people felt that to Trek from this point was their only salvation whilst others, like ourselves, were not so sure. It was a very troubled night for the adults in our party for they knew that whatever decision they made, would mean life or death to us all and as no assurance could be truthfully offered, each one knew that their choice would involve a gamble with fate.

Early the next morning my Mother got us together and told us that we were leaving for Sumprabum but that my Father's brother and family and also my other Aunt and her two small girls, had decided to attempt the Trek from the 102nd mile point. It seemed that all the other refugees had made a similar choice for we were alone in deciding to go up to the village of Sumprabum. There was a tearful farewell and we left with the first light of day, heavy of heart and still not knowing what lay in store for us.

We were once again filled with the fear of undertaking this journey, treacherous as it was - this time with my Uncle Jim's car and a discarded Ford which my Brother Victor drove. This was only possible because my Brothers had managed to collect petrol in several discarded bottles and cans from the many abandoned vehicles scattered around in the mud. Neither vehicle was in MOT condition so, many prayers were added to the petrol!

A view from the hills around Sumprabum

It took us nearly a week to reach Sumprabum - which lay in the mist some three and a half thousand feet above the Mali Hka Valley, nestled below the Kumon Range of mountains in the Kachin hills of northern Burma. From here there was a cart track which led to the outpost called Fort Hertz, beyond which there were several mountain ranges, gorges and impassable streams. We were now in an area between China and Assam with Tibet on the horizon. For a while we just sat on a hill slope glad to be resting in the peaceful surroundings of this pretty village, after the turmoil of the past months. Understandably, our first reaction was to prefer that we settle here for the duration of the war although it must be said that this preference was based on uncertainty and a great deal of fear as to the outcome of another choice.

However, many factors were to be considered in making a decision. The main factor being, the threat of the Japanese Army reaching this outpost which could have been used by them for Military purposes in their further quest for occupying Assam and then India - who knows! Our fate would then be in their hands and from all accounts our chances of remaining unharmed remote. Once again it seemed that we could waste no time in making the decision which was to take us on the most perilous venture of our lives.

We unloaded our belongings and settled ourselves in a Government Bungalow, relieved at having reached our temporary destination. The luxury of a bath and a hot meal of sorts, after so much travelling, were more than welcome. By now the sun was setting and from our hilltop position, we were treated to a Panoramic view of the hills surrounding this little village - a truly beautiful sight which did not harbour well within our troubled minds at this point. The evening air was becoming quite chill and so a fire was lit, as was customary in this hilly country. We children were sent to bed in an adjoining room while the grownups sat around the fire, mugs of tea in their hands, deep in conversation, weighing up the dangers attached to each of the choices to be made.

CHAPTER SEVEN

"Our Gurkha friend Mr Bhadu"

Although we were expected to be asleep, sleep would not come for we were old enough to know that things were happening and be caught up in the anxious confusion. From the darkness of our rooms my sister Patsy and I would peep in on the scene next door and notice that from time to time my Uncle and brothers were missing. We later noticed a strange low voice having joined in the talk and on investigating found that a soldier in military uniform had joined in the "pow wow". He was to greatly influence our ultimate decision for, by now, we had made a preferred choice of settling in Sumprabum. We planned to live as the natives did, off the land, praying that the Japanese army would find the journey over those 150 difficult miles not worth their trouble!

However, the stranger in question was a Gurkha Sergeant who with his family were occupying a small Bungalow close to where we were. He had travelled around this area considerably, in the course of his peacetime duties and, what's more, knew the Kachin dialect. This man, whom we were to know as Mr. Bhadu, did not share our optimism about the Japanese not venturing this far north and by now stories had reached us of the maltreatment handed out by the Japanese to the British. I realise now that our Gurkha friend had as much reason to not want to fall into their hands. Besides having a wife and eight children ranging in age from 6 months to 15 years, the mere fact of him being a Gurkha soldier would have jeopardised his chances of survival.

History tells us that the Japanese did in fact take the war against the British into the Kachin Hills so our options were as known to us and the outcome, if having chosen to stay, will forever remain unanswered.

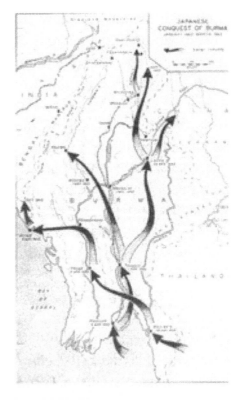

This map indicates the Japanese conquest of Burma Jan 1942 – Mar 1942 and extended to the Kachin Hills

This discussion went on into the early hours of the morning and each time our sleep was disturbed, we would note that the fire burned brightly and the family were still sitting around talking in low voices. The possibility of following up rumours that there may still have been airlifts to India from a small airstrip at Putao in the Fort Hertz settlement north of Sumprabum, were discussed. However, the memory of what happened at Myitkyina was still too fresh in our minds for my Uncle and Mother to even consider such a gamble. In any event the only means of reaching this point would, we were told, have been by Elephant - a terrifying prospect in this hilly country.

During one of my eavesdropping periods I heard Mr Bhadu tell my Uncle and Mother that he knew of a route across the hills which, though dangerous and difficult, would take us to India in about 'TEN DAYS' time. However impossible this must have sounded to my Mother and Uncle, it was hope to cling to and it sounded distinctly preferable to becoming Japanese prisoners of war. Given the nature of our family group and the reports that had reached us concerning the treatment we might expect, this caused us to doubt the wisdom of our previous choice.

At this point I drifted into sleep and woke to find the sun shining through the Bungalow window. My sister Patsy and myself noticed that my Mother was not lying by our side as she had always done since leaving our home and so we went in search of her. We found her sitting on the Bungalow steps, seemingly admiring the sunrise but when we joined her, she hugged us to her so intently that we could sense the anxiety she felt on our account. She must have been so troubled and anxious stepping out into the unknown with us so young and fearing the untold dangers which lay ahead. She was also very anxious concerning my brother Frank who was only just recovering from his serious illness at Myitkyina.

That morning we all sat down to a breakfast of eggs obtained from the village and fried tinned meats, with a locally baked form of bread made of unrefined maize, which could have been left by previous officials who travelled this road on Government duty. This was to be our last decent meal for months to come.

After breakfast my Mother told us that my Uncle and she had decided that we try and walk to India and that although it would be over rough country, it wouldn't take very long!! She told us that we had someone going with us who knew the area and that it only meant us being rationed to a certain amount of food each day. In this way it was hoped that the supplies of grain and tinned food which they had got together from the Bungalow and the village would last through that ten-day journey. To my thirteen-year-old sister Patsy and myself, this sounded more the promise of an exciting adventure and after all there were ample grown-ups to take care of us so we were not unduly anxious!

My Uncle had instructed each of us to get together a small bundle of our most needy possessions, a change of clothing and us young ones were to carry a blanket each while the older ones carried as much as they could, including a small supply of quinine and aspirin. I must admit that I was very optimistic as to my physical strength for I had, childlike, packed all manner of things in my bundle. This was to prove far too heavy but my dear Mother knew that it would be kinder to permit this at the start knowing in her heart that before long I would be compelled to discard most of those 'treasures' I had so carefully chosen.

I was broken hearted to have to leave my cat 'Blacky' behind but my Mother explained to me that he would get lost in the jungle and starve to death whereas the local people in Sumprabum would look after him. My cat had travelled with us from Myitkyina in a basket, mostly on my lap, never wandering far from me when we stopped. It was, as my Father always said - a most unusual cat - who had originally travelled to Burma by ship from England and was found by my Dad's workmen when unloading supplies in Syriam. He was in fact a 'stowaway'. I became very attached to Blacky, as he was to me. Many tears were shed parting from him.

CHAPTER EIGHT

"The Kachin Bearers"

So it was that on the sunlit morning of May 12th, 1942, our little band of twenty hopefuls set forth from Sumprabum, so optimistic in our ignorance, heading westwards towards the forbidding, jungle clad slopes of the Kumon Range. We had managed to hire three Kachin bearers, one was to carry my Grandmother and the other two to act as Guides and carry our food and other necessities such as the Army groundsheet which had been given to us at the 102nd mile post. We also took with us a large brown cooking pot which was to serve us throughout the Trek. There were some enamel plates and mugs gained from the Bungalow at Sumprabum - no doubt Army Issue - which also served us well.

On reflection I wished we had kept this cooking pot which so often afforded us the only saving comfort at the end of each tortuous day - a hot drink to warm out chilled hearts and bodies. However, it could be that, at our journeys end, the older members of the family wished to retain nothing of the nightmare we had endured, praying that we would find the strength to recover fully and put it all behind us some day!

My Brother Frank, though still weak, refused the option of a Kachin bearer in favour of more pressing needs and was determined to try and walk with the rest of us. My Mother, especially, remained ever watchful of his progress and whenever possible gave him priority with any nourishment on offer! I should mention the amazing way in which the Kachin bearers carried their loads, human or otherwise, by securing them to a Bamboo frame resting on their backs but being supported by a strong band worn over their foreheads.

In the case of my Grandmother, the frame was made in such a way as to allow a narrow seat about ten inches wide which meant that it was far from comfortable. Besides, the effect of always travelling in a backward direction was very unnerving, and kept her in a permanent state of fear. She would be facing the sky for the most part, as the bearer would naturally need to distribute the weight of his passenger by walking in a stooped position, especially when climbing hills. No doubt looking up to the sky directed her fears to God whose help she constantly cried out for. As I write, my heart aches in thinking of her poor frightened mind, made more acute by her age and condition.

We were soon to realise how physically strong these Kachin people were on a diet which, by our normal standards, was far from balanced. I do not remember any Kachin being overweight, due, no doubt, to their diet and constant exercise in negotiating their homeland hills.

CHAPTER NINE

"The Monsoons and our Jungle Tormentors"

We were trekking through an area in the world which experiences the worst Monsoon flooding and the timing could not have been worse. It is during the months of May to October that the Monsoons prevail and it was during these months that we were undertaking this journey. For the first day or two, our path had taken us down the comparatively gentle slopes of Sumprabum itself and with some food, dry blankets and clothing, we felt no more than a strange tiredness of limb. At the end of each day we were more than ready to wrap ourselves in our blankets and fall asleep at sunset huddled together on the ground sheet under cover of tree branches so deftly put together by our Kachin guides. My Mother would always choose the best available spot for our Grandmother, Patsy, and myself, although we made sure she was always very close to us. The strength and comfort she exuded, from her slight frame, was truly exceptional, as we were to bear witness to in the months ahead.

Mr. Bhadu and his family would settle themselves similarly a few yards away for, at this stage, we were keen on each family choosing for ourselves a little privacy as far as possible. Our supplies were also packed and carried separately, each being responsible for the payment of their own bearers. The struggle of this little family touched our hearts for so many of them were very young and it meant the older brother and sisters carrying the little ones. Never did we hear them complain although tears flowed freely at times, as it did with us.

The next week or so found our path taking us deeper and deeper into thick Jungle heading in a north-westerly direction towards the Chaukan Pass, climbing very high Mountain Ridges to 8000ft high in places. Many of us were by this time suffering high fevers and the ague of Malaria when our whole bodies would shake uncontrollably. The monsoons made sure that we no longer carried dry clothing and were ourselves soaked whilst trekking. The wet jungle brought out one of our most constant tormentors - the tropical leech - which clung to us as we were forced to brush through the dank undergrowth. These thready creatures would in wormlike fashion hoist their heads, in a swaying motion, seemingly choosing their next point of attack, when they would feast on our blood till they had become too heavy to retain their gum like adhesion.

This unfamiliar hazard caused us a great deal of physical pain, making us dread each step we took, knowing that we would be covered in them as we fought our way through the thick undergrowth. There was no time to stop and remove them all, for it was imperative that we keep pace as far as possible, with our guides, to whom leeches were an accepted co-heir to these jungle clad hills. The Kachins carried sharp knives which they used so deftly for every imaginable purpose, including the disposal of a particularly stubborn leech by merely slicing off the outer layer of skin to which the leech was attached! Their feet were, of course, hardened to cope, with them constantly treading these tortuous jungle paths barefooted. We, on the other hand, suffered unimaginable agony trekking barefooted through all these jungle hazards. We were soon to become aware of the many jungle inhabitants who were to threaten our every move and fill us with fear which remained with us throughout the Trek.

Fortunately, my Uncle had brought with him a small supply of silver money which was the only payment acceptable to these Kachin guides. They would stay with us from one village to the next when they would hand us over to new guides. At this stage of the Trek, we were near enough our point of departure to be within reach of the encroaching Japanese army, so perhaps their own safety would have required that they not be found helping us escape. I am not sure as to the extent of their awareness of what being overrun by the Japanese Army would mean to them. Whereas the route we were following ensured that we were never really 'lost' in Kachin terms, at this stage, it did not guarantee that we maintain a westward course. We were nevertheless entirely dependent on these guides, more so as we progressed further into the dense jungle. In any event we were now trekking through previously un-negotiated terrain as confirmed to us by Mr. Bhadu.

I should mention here that my Uncle had brought two Rifles and a pistol, in anticipation of having to defend ourselves against the terrors of the jungle and any hostility we may encounter from the 'uncivilised tribes', through whose domain we would have to travel. This gave my two brothers and himself a firearm each and Mr. Bhadu had also brought a rifle and a small supply of bullets. In addition to the money and firearms, my Uncle had, through years of experience in the Government Excise Department, learned just how useful a bargaining weapon opium was with these people. With this in mind, he had somehow secured a small quantity for such an emergency before leaving Sumprabum. We were to appreciate its immense medicinal value later on.

CHAPTER TEN

"The Kachin Villages"

By the end of the first week we had passed through two Kachin villages and were grateful for the shelter they afforded us from the horrors of the jungle. These Kachin huts were erected on stilts made of bamboo which was also used for the floors, whilst the walls and roof were of thatch. The huts were long and narrow and there would be two or three crude fireplaces, spaced at intervals down the centre. Here the food was cooked and the family gathered at the end of each day to smoke a communal pipe and exchange the day's gossip. I use the word "family" in the broadest sense. The fireplaces were no more than a firmly pressed damp mud base on which a wood fire was lit and the continual smouldering of damp wood meant that these huts were constantly filled with thick smoke. It is not surprising considering that the small entrance door mostly afforded the only light and ventilation for each hut.

At first the smoke troubled us greatly but of necessity we accustomed ourselves to it. We now knew why these people smelt of smoke.

At the entrance of the hut there would be a crudely made grain pounder where it seemed the older women of the village were constantly employed. Whereas their rules of hygiene would certainly not conform to ours, they would subject their children to frequent dousing, if the water supply was near enough to the village. There was always nature's water supply in plenty at this time of the year. We noted that the women seemed to do most of the work, whilst caring for their young, who were strapped to their backs and remained there throughout the day. They worked in the fields, fetched wood for the fires and generally managed everything. The men it seemed were enjoying all the privileges of pre-emancipation days, assuming the role of hunter and master!

Although they were never openly hostile, with us being the first white people they had encountered, they remained shyly aloof and we could see that in spite of our attempts to be friendly, they were somewhat suspicious of us. However, as I write I realise that those of us who survived owed our lives to these quiet, strong, gentle people without whose help we would have perished. I remember them with immense gratitude and pray that they remain able to retain their peaceful appreciation of life.

They would vacate a corner of one of their huts to give us shelter and whilst we had items which we could barter, we managed to get some fresh food. A little locally grown rice and pumpkin with an occasional chicken obtained in exchange for some prized piece of jewellery. In our present circumstance values had altered completely and anything we possessed was valueless, other than what it could be exchanged for, to assist our survival.

Now well into the second week of our trek we were facing another very steep mountain ridge of the Kumon range. Our sore feet made our steps less buoyant and our clothing clung to our bodies. We were chilled to our bones. However, with my dear Mother's constant encouragement we were still fairly optimistic thinking that, having surmounted this mountain range, we would be within sight of our goal and the end of all this suffering.

It was as well that we did not realise the exact direction of our route or the perilous country through which we would yet have to trek. Perhaps knowing this at that early stage, would have tempted us to give in to the Malaria, which had already struck nearly every member of our group. Walking in these conditions, often with a high fever, meant that our progress was painfully slow at times. At the end of the day, those of us who were able, took a little 'nourishment' from a can of soup shared between as many as possible. We were now having to get used to the near starvation which formed part of our lives for the next five months.

The jungle swamps attracted the most deadly species of mosquito and we had little or no protection against them, for the very small amount of quinine tablets which we had set out with had, by now, been reduced to no more than an emergency supply. Our pace had naturally slowed to that of the least able amongst us for, although the decrease in our food supplies had left us an extra bearer to carry the sick, the question was, who was the most incapable of carrying on, for we were nearly all sick people.

My Mother's natural preference was that my sister Patsy be carried since she was in a high malarial fever and quite unable to stand, let alone walk. By now, we were travelling so slowly that it took us days to get from one Kachin village to the next, always remembering that we were of course climbing steep mountain sides, made dangerously slippery by the rain soaked leaves which covered the ground. So it was that we spent many nights camped in dense jungle, with but a small area cleared to give us a spot to put up our faithful groundsheet, providing some cover from the rain. The other sheet was spread on the bracken which had been hurriedly cleared to base this shelter. Most days, we could hardly wait to throw ourselves down on a small spot, exhausted, wet, cold, hungry and so often in a high fever. It was at these points that we felt the hopelessness of our plight and the temptation to give in was greatest.

However, at each sunrise we would have to muster enough courage to set out again following our guides who found ways of keeping themselves going till they handed us over to the next village whenever that could be reached. The Kachins would lead in a sure-footed fashion, borne no doubt from having trod these mountain paths since early childhood. As our only interpreter was Mr. Bhadu, whose party were not always immediately by our group, we had to soon resort to an exchange of ideas in sign language which worked to some extent. Although the Kachins never attempted to harm us in any way, they never showed much sign of being friendly either, but this we later judged to be more a characteristic of these people than a reflection of hostility. They were possibly anxious as to what ill effects they may suffer, confronting for the first time in their case, the danger of contracting illnesses for which they had not developed an immunity, within their segregated life style. No doubt in most cases we were the first white people they had met so they must have felt unsure of our presence although our physical state must have assured them that we were no threat, just grateful to them for our survival!

On reaching the village of Shakyu Ga, we were compelled to rest for a day or two because so many of us were inflicted with a high fever. The many leech bites on our bodies were turning into infected sores and from having slept in these natives huts, our heads were full of lice. To my Mother, who had always insisted on the strictest rules for personal and household cleanliness, these conditions and, above all seeing us thus infected, must have dealt a crushing blow to her brave heart. Now, as in the dark days ahead, she insisted that we never allow ourselves to be reduced to the state of our surroundings. Our hair was cut as short as possible but for some reason my Mother was reluctant to part with hers and, for a while yet, wore it in a bun.

In spite of all the hardships we suffered in these huts, they were infinitely preferable to the horrors we were exposed to in the jungle. Here at least we had shelter from the torrential rain, leeches and the ever present danger of wild animals. However, we knew that to rest more than was absolutely necessary could prove fatal and Mr. Bhadu had warned us that, if we did not move faster, we could be trapped between rivers made impassable by the monsoon swell. So, having somewhat replenished our food supply by buying a little locally grown rice and vegetables we moved on - albeit at a slow pace.

CHAPTER ELEVEN

"Facing the Forbidding Kumon Range"

Kumon Range of Mountains

On leaving this village, we headed in a north westerly direction along the Kumon Range climbing and descending mountains in some cases 4000ft high, with all the frightening hazards attached and from then on there were no villages till we reached the Hukawng Valley. This meant that we would have to subsist on the food we carried, which was very little and have to camp in the jungle at the end of each day. We had only a few tins of condensed milk left and this was kept for the weakest among us. Our medical supplies had also been reduced to no more than a thermometer, small bottle of aspirin tablets, a few quinine tablets and a packet of permanganate of potassium! These were wholly inadequate for our pressing needs but by now, we had, through my dear Mother's example, learned to use prayer as a supplement for medicine!

Mr. Bhadu's family had also fallen prey to Malaria fever, stomach disorders, sores, and fatigue, with himself, his wife and two older children each carrying one of the younger ones. I shall always remember the quiet courage of Mrs. Bhadu who must have felt deeply for the suffering of her children at their tender age but who always seemed to smile at us when we showed sympathy for her little ones. We at least had each other to talk to but, with her not knowing sufficient English, she was only able to talk to her husband and children. Mr Bhadu was, of course, so often busily engaged in making vital decisions with my Uncle. His knowledge of the Kachin language and customs proved of tremendous value to us.

We were now in dense jungle and there was no turning back for we had crossed rivers which would now be impassable because of the monsoons. The going was very rough and we had encountered the near impossibility of climbing these very high slime covered mountain slopes, which, in places, were so steep that we had to attempt them on all fours. The monsoons had turned vast areas of this terrain into swamps and quagmire. The thick Bamboo growth which covered so much of the valleys between the mountains, made losing one's foothold even more perilous. Besides the depth of the fall, there would have been no hope of surviving a drop on these razor sharp bamboo blades. We were to have many narrow escapes in this way.

The nature of the paths we were now treading meant that our pace was restrained to a bare crawl in places and in this way, it took us nearly a month to cover the next forty miles or so to the Chaukan Pass, walking from sunrise to sunset. Our pace was restricted to that of the weakest of our group. We were climbing high mountains lashed by heavy rain and we were perilously cold at the height we were at. Our clothing was totally inappropriate for our needs and there was nothing to assure us that every step we took would bring us nearer to the end of our suffering. Could we have been forgiven for thinking that God could not have been looking down on this patch of jungle!

This past week or two had proved to be the hardest so far. We were following no set path, just walking deeper into the jungle, not seeing the sky for most of the day. At lower levels the steamy heat of the dank undergrowth drained us of the little energy we managed to muster. The rain poured down incessantly and our bodies, so weakened by fever and fatigue, were in no shape to tramp these deadly mountainous tracks. One or other of the grownups in our group frequently questioned the wisdom of our choice in attempting this perilous trek! How hard it was to believe that God could hear our prayers but we somehow trusted my Mother's faith and kept asking for miracles. The swollen rivers we were forced to cross in the most primitive and dangerous ways.

At this stage my Mother had developed an abscess in her ear which caused her to be in a high fever and for the first time she needed to be carried by bearer. To us, somehow, this seemed the beginning of the end for seeing my Mother being carried in this way, barely conscious, brought to mind for the first time, the very real fear of death. Up to now it had been suffering - but with survival as the outcome!

I remember sitting where I was, soaked and covered in leeches, too miserable to care what happened to me. My eldest sister Joyce and brother Victor forced me up, practically dragging me bodily, crying as I was, and without sympathizing, ushering me on. This was to be the way, time and time again, I realize now how hard this must have been for them but they were aware that self-pity was as much to be guarded against as were the dangers surrounding us. They knew that even at my young age I would have to call upon all my inner strength and determination to survive. The condition of each member of the family meant that we were unable to offer each other much physical help, though I feel sure that our affection and concern for each other provided the blanket support needed to keep us going.

With my Mother having to be carried, my sister Patsy was now walking somewhat slightly recovered but still extremely weak. We would try and support each other but the nature of our surroundings was such that for the most part we trekked in single file order, with the two Kachins leading. Our physical condition made progress painfully slow. Patsy and myself seemed to spend most of our rest periods trying to rid ourselves of leeches which were everywhere. This sometimes meant rubbing them off on to each other! I had become a little more used to these "blood relatives" of ours but Patsy would become hysterical at the presence of them on her head or around her face. The irony of our situation was that in peacetime we were never exposed to 'creepy crawlies' of any kind and would make an awful fuss at having to deal with them. Here we were totally infested with all manner of 'insectile' beings!

We had now reached the Chaukan Pass which meant that we were at the summit of a mountain in the 11,000-ft, range.

It was cold and in our condition breathing at this altitude became difficult. Besides, the ground on which we were to make camp was a sodden mass but as this was the only flat ground on which we could camp, before attempting the perilous descent, we had no option but to settle ourselves here as best we could. We were all in a sorry state, both physically and mentally on arrival here and the surrounding conditions did nothing to give our hearts a lift.

However, as there was no time to lose before sunset, those of us who could summon enough strength, helped make a clearing, our primary concern being to arrange a fairly dry spot on which my Mother and Grandmother could lie. We had filled the boggy areas with branches but this meant that there was no way of keeping away the jungle pests which were now beneath and around us!

The Kachin Guides helped stack four poles in the ground and to this we tried weaving a shelter of branches which, though welcome as temporary relief, soon proved inadequate for the heavy rain that seemed to beat down on us continuously. The sound of that rain and the screams of the jungle so overtook our subconscious that it was a very long time before we could 'listen in' to the world around us without hearing those screams and sounds. For that matter neither were we able to rid ourselves of the smells of the jungle for a long time.

Under this part cover, we had laid a ground sheet and settled my Mother and Grandmother, striving to keep off the rain and wet which seemed everywhere. Our blankets were soaked and it was nearly impossible to get a fire going in these conditions. Nevertheless my dear Sister Phyllis and Gloria did eventually manage to get a small fire burning, using anything combustible, so that they could heat some water to make a cup of Kachin tea. Although this was not so appealing to our taste, it did provide a hot drink which warmed our chilled bodies.

We began to realise that when nothing is the option a very little of 'something' is immeasurable! At this point I remember experiencing the agony of contact with nettles, in the jungles surrounding us, when trying to find a secluded spot for personal needs. The agony remains in my memory and the antidote, when found, took long to bring relief. Nettles were, of course, another ever present threat to us. The jungles were full of them.

In these wet conditions we could not attempt much other cooking so in addition to our other torments, we were to be deprived of our meagre sustenance. My Mother was by this time in chronic pain and to have to sit by and see her suffer in this way, tore our hearts from us. Eventually my Uncle decided that we should give her a little of the opium he carried with him and in this way, sleep overtook her at the height of her agony. We huddled close together, trying to keep warm, and especially to keep my Mother and Grandmother as warm as possible, praying all the while, although our present plight made us momentarily wonder whether our prayers were drowned by the screams of the jungle!

None of us could sleep that night for we were too cold, wet and worried on my Mother's account, so when dawn came we were relieved, though far from ready to start out on a day's hard march. Looking down on what lay ahead, filled us with fear and so it was that at this point I remember us giving in to tears, screaming our surrender to the hills! The older members of our family had begun to question choices being made and it seemed that we were all defying death but would it not have been preferable to our present plight!

With my Mother still being in a high fever and others of us in the party suffering frequent bouts of malarial ague, we had to remain in that "hell" for another day. We were glad of a chance to rest but the word rest was only applicable in the sense that we were not walking. It was impossible to sleep, fatigued though we were, for we were chilled to our bones with no means of warming ourselves. The rain beat down on us mercilessly. The dank undergrowth surrounding us harboured all manner of snakes, leeches, spiders etc., so our safety required that we be alert to the dangers of the jungle.

CHAPTER TWELVE

"Cobra Alert"

It was on the second day of our stop at this Pass, that we were to once again resort to prayer in our dire need. My Uncle, Mr. Bhadu and Victor, with our two Guides, had gone to survey the best path to choose when making our descent the following day. As was so often the case, there were no set paths in this mountainous territory so it was a case of choosing a trail which appeared less forbidding - to start with at any rate. Very often our trail would lead us to impossible jungle depths and we would have to retrace our steps - diverting our course.

We girls were seated around my Mother and Grandmother, trying to administer comfort if not relief from pain. My Mother appeared to be asleep at last and we were about to settle ourselves by her side when we were alerted at the sound of a heavy thud coming from the direction of the undergrowth, near where my Mother's head lay.

Frozen in the fear of what we saw, we could barely open our lips to pray for the miracle we hoped for. There coiled in a heap, within a few feet of my Mother's head was a huge snake which we took to be a deadly Cobra, head erect seemingly poised to deliver a fatal thrust. Instead, as if uninterested in its surroundings, this potential killer turned and slid away back into the undergrowth.

My mother being partly asleep and partly under the numbing effects of opium, was mercifully unaware of what had happened. However, instead of this being the 'parthian shot' to our hopes, it gave us renewed spirit for we had surely witnessed a miracle and now felt even more willing to place our hands in those of the miracle worker! The presence of snakes in such close proximity left us fearful and unable to close our eyes that night - waiting for dawn!

Again, as if by a further miracle, my Mother awoke the next morning and said her ear was better and that she felt weak but much more able to continue. We could hardly believe the change in her and rushed to provide a drink of Kachin Tea to warm her - Phyllis and Gloria using any strength left to encourage the embers of our fire to produce this. She hugged us to her and from this we gained so much comfort as always. We apportioned the Kachin Bearer to carry my Mother with my Brother Victor and myself helping Patsy to walk.

We began the descent of this mountainous region, only to find that another lay before us. Our Kachin guides, having surveyed the hilly nature of this area and knowing that they were far from their homes and not within sight of other Kachin villages, decided to change course. This involved re-tracing several of the miles which we had so recently gained through supreme physical effort and endurance. However, we had no option but to follow the guides whose primitive navigational instincts were all we had to depend on. They were no doubt more aware than we were of the dangerous terrain we were facing

Most of us had lost our shoes at the beginning of the Trek in boggy marshes or in crossing a mountain torrent and we were now treading these jungle paths bare footed, this being agony enough in itself. It seemed now that our direction was to follow the rivers, as far as possible, between each mountain Range.

The rivers which we were following had their source in mountain streams and further swelled by the monsoon floods, had gathered force, turning them into rushing torrents. In attempting to cross these rivers the usual procedure was for us to form a human chain. The two Kachins would lead and the more able members of the party place themselves in a position order which would enable them to help those of us who could not manage on our own.

Recalling these crossings brings to mind the awful fear we experienced at each attempt. There was much screaming and our shredded nerves sometimes caused us to doubt each other. As I write I realise just how much we relied on the strength of our love and trust of each other in coping with these impossible odds.

Most often the water was up to my shoulders and there was no way of knowing to what depth the next step would take us. Sometimes crossing on foot was impossible and the only way left open to us was to crawl on our stomachs along the trunk of a tree, which the Kachins had felled for the purpose. With hearts and bodies practically paralysed with fear we would inch our way over, never daring to open our eyes, till we felt the comfort of hands reached out to help us to safety. Beneath us was the sound of rushing water which was very frightening. In dealing with such situations we were always compelled to look ahead and never look back and this could be applied to so many aspects of this dangerous and tortuous experience of our lives.

CHAPTER THIRTEEN

"The Elephants"

Whilst being guided from one village to the next, rivers were sometimes crossed by Bamboo Suspension bridges. These were put together by the Kachins in a somewhat primitive fashion - no doubt suitable enough for their needs. However, in our state of mind, we were afraid that it may not have proved negotiable, given the physical condition of most of our group. Necessity dictated that we follow the only option and so it was that, with several mishaps and anxious moments, we did traverse these rain swelled torrents in this way, on many occasions. We soon learned that in our predicament giving in to fear meant surrendering our hope of survival, which we were not yet prepared to do. I remember my Mother telling me that there were two kinds of fear i.e. 'Good fear' which acted as a warning of dangers and 'Bad fear' which took away your hope! I must admit that all of us must have experienced a bit of both on this Trek!

We were now about thirty miles south of the Chaukan Pass, heading in a south westerly direction, following the Tawang Hka River and having crossed endless jungle clad mountain ranges, we were relieved to find that the mountains were becoming less steep. We were soon overlooking a valley which appeared to stretch for miles and miles. Our pace was still limited by our poor physical condition and the treacherous nature of the hillsides down which we were painfully treading. We were afraid to lose our footing for this could have meant disaster, as it often did. Further injury and near loss of life was par for the course during this perilous descent. I clearly remember my poor Sister Phyllis experiencing this danger at this point and can picture my descent to where she had fallen amidst screams of fear. For once our screams easily matched those of the jungle creatures around us. The terrors of the jungle swamped our every move and we began to accept the proximity of death more readily as we faced each more threatening stage.

The sight of one or two Kachin villages in the valley below cheered us up a little for it brought the promise of food. Since our meagre supply had been exhausted we were looking forward to such a promise with hopeful hearts. By now we had been reduced to but shadows of our former selves, hardly recognisable to each other and too weak to care! Our small supply of salt with which we had set out, was soon consumed and from then on anything we ate was without salt, which made us realise just how necessary it is to one's appreciation of food. We did come upon a Salt Lake in the Kumon Range from where we obtained some crude salt stone. However, even in our desperate need, it proved no substitute.

It was near this Salt Lake that we encountered wild animals which often came too near for comfort but for some reason never did attack us. One night which I particularly remember was a night when we were camped on a river bank, huddled together trying to keep warm and we heard this heavy treading coming from across the water. Being a moonlit night we soon recognised the forms of Elephants, about five or six in all. We were naturally terrified because the river at this point was quite shallow, and could easily have been negotiated by them.

Decisions were being made in whispers - the party not being able to agree on a course of action. Eventually, it was decided that we try and get a fire going and make as loud a 'clanging noise' as possible with the empty tins and cooking pot we had. The Elephants did not seem too concerned over our 'performance', merely completing their mission which was to refresh themselves with drink and make their way back. Many prayers were said - in thanks - that night.

It seemed that there were laws to be observed even in the depths of the jungle and the elephants were not going to be offenders without provocation! This was more or less the pattern of events each time we encountered wild animals and we learned to respect their rights, since we were most surely intruders of their habitat. This meant that whilst we were often exposed to and fearful of the dangers of facing wild animals in the terrain through which we were trekking, we maintained a deep respect for the inhabitants of the jungle. We remained ever watchful and observant of the caution shown by our native guides whose experience in treading these jungle paths was to be our salvation.

We were climbing paths that did not exist and descending steep hillsides void of paths and clearings. Somehow our overall condition and plight brought this fear to an acceptable level which we faced with a certain degree of fatalism. It was the smaller 'occupants' of the jungle who caused us the most pain and torture it seemed.

Our self-respect and personal hygiene were being maintained under the most bizarre of circumstances throughout this Trek. We were compelled to carry out bodily functions under the most harrowing of conditions, so often exposing ourselves to the dangers of the jungle in preference to losing what little dignity we retained. There were to be many instances where our preference nearly cost us our lives. It was perhaps this very choice, small though it was within the framework of our fight for survival, which kept us from being reduced to the level of our circumstances. In the days that followed we were to witness how the suffering and trauma of this terrible Trek was to strip thousands of people of their will to remain civilized in these conditions and thus lose their fight to survive. They could never be blamed for this!

Once again it was through my Mother's insistence that we fulfilled day to day conventional habits, as far as our frail bodies and minds could muster the strength for. Whilst these may have appeared ludicrous in our surroundings we realised that, to have attempted to rub our teeth and gums with the type of jungle stick used by the Kachins, was useful in keeping our gums and mouths 'clean'. We were well washed by the monsoon rains, our small supply of soap being frugally shared till there was nothing left. My sister Joyce carried a small bag which was to become very precious to us. It contained our only pair of small scissors, tweezers (which were in constant use removing the leeches and many thorns which entered our flesh as we walked in these jungles) and a packet of needles and thread which were to prove so useful in so many circumstances throughout the trek.

We had reached the village of Ngalang Ga, about the third week of June and the effects of the past six weeks horror was taking its toll of even the strongest amongst the party. We were now reduced to a band of weary, footsore, starved refugees who had succumbed to Malaria fever, stomach disorders, septic sores, cuts, bruises and many other diseases which would have been considered serious under normal conditions. It seemed that whatever physical resistance we had shown at first was fast being drained from us. Whereas at first we were glad of anything to satisfy our hunger, now it did not seem so important that we be satisfied!

Oh how we longed to rest and not go any further! However, my dear Mother knew that to rest now would mean surrendering our will to fight and so with her unassailable courage she forced us to keep going, pray and not lose hope. Our Rosary beads were forever entwined in our fingers and, whenever we had the strength to do so, we would, with my Mother leading, recite these prayers as we forced our weary legs on. On reflection, our prayers had become constant pleas for help rather than conventional ones but I'm sure God heard them for any of us to have survived our ordeal!

Reflecting on this today I realise just how mentally strong I had become during this trek to override the deficiency of my years in coping with it as I did. My dear sister Patsy - though 1 year 8 months older than me had, under these circumstances, succumbed to illness and weakness from the early stages of the trek. She was having to be cared for, as far as possible, whilst I seemed to have been able to follow my Mother's lead in fighting the odds. My eldest sister found my acceptance of our circumstances unbelievable, given my age and I remember her once telling my Father, in later years, that she marvelled at my strength of heart and mind. I just thank God that he had given me this strength to survive and so enjoy the rest of my life with all its blessings.

CHAPTER FOURTEEN

"The Hukawng Valley"

A less formidable trekking path!

We noticed at this point that the streams we were following did not flow as quickly, nor were the slopes of the hills so steep. The jungle itself was gradually thinning out and we realised that we were entering the valley which we had looked down on from the Chaukan Pass. Whilst we had so often dreamed of the sheer relief of walking on even ground, we were not to find such relief. It seemed that the perils of the mountains had merely been replaced by the agony of walking through mile upon mile of grass, at least five feet high, more in places, with razor like edges which cut into our flesh at every step. It seemed that in spite of being exposed to so much hardship, our skins were still without the hardened resistance of the Kachin skin and we suffered much from this new torture. I remember thinking at this stage that if we ever did come out of this alive, I would buy myself a pair of padded silk slippers!

However, being in the plains, it was easier to follow the course of the rivers than it was in the mountain region. We were now entering the Hukawng Valley, a name which is forever imprinted on my heart and mind. On arrival at the first village in this valley we were to encounter our one and only sign of hostility from the natives. It had been another day of heavy rain and we were all longing for the shelter of a Kachin hut with all its drawbacks and, not having ever been refused shelter of some sort, were not prepared for the reception we received.

Although Mr. Bhadu did his best to reassure these villagers that we wanted no more than that we rest for a night in the shelter of one of their huts, they were not impressed by our need. Much haggling took place and we noticed more sharp blades at their sides than usual. My Uncle, spoke of us not showing fear and whilst not acting in an aggressive way made no attempt to hide the rifle and revolver he had with him. By now we had very little money left and only sufficient opium for chronic medicinal needs, so there was no hope of bartering our way.

Having kept us in suspense for quite a while, during which time we were becoming ever more wet and cold, they agreed to escort us to a hut at the far end of the village. Judging by the spectral atmosphere of this hut and the unwholesome relics lying around, this was the hut which was used for burial rites and ceremonies - perhaps! We were later told that this was an ante room of the Kachin Nat House – the Kachin Nat House was a place of reverence to the spirits of the dead. A prayer room of sorts. Needless to say, we were not to enjoy a very restful night, but at least we were sheltered from the elements and able to make ourselves a hot drink of sorts. We left early the next morning, in the pouring rain not wishing to outstay our "welcome"! Mr. Bhadu confirmed that we were the first white people they had encountered!

We continued following the Tanai Hka River and camped on its banks that night. Both my Mother and sister Patsy were very ill at this point and that night proved one of particular significance to my eldest sister Joyce, who later suffered much as a result of it.

There we were lying on near wet blankets on the sand bank of this river, with only the ground sheet supported on bamboo poles, acting as a part shelter against the heavy rain. We were sitting or lying in pools of water, being bitten to death by sand flies - a new tormentor. My sister Joyce saw that night through in a cramped position with Patsy lying on her outstretched legs and my Mother's head on her lap, both raving in the delirium of a high fever. I was crouching close to them, trying to keep off the rain and applying a wet cloth to their fevered brows. Sadly, I remember telling Joyce that it would be good if we could all die together on that Sandbank! She kissed me and cried. The rest of the family were camped in similar conditions in another 'makeshift shelter' a few yards away, suffering as we were. With dawn came the realisation that we had reached a stage when few of us could walk any further.

Being in such poor physical shape, we were relieved to be able to resort to two Kachin 'dug outs'. These we obtained through our Kachin guides, who had fetched them out of the bordering jungle. They knew where to look for them since the Kachins apparently used the River as a 'Road' for their own purposes. So we were able to float down the river to the next village which was a few miles downstream. We set out, completely unaware of what lay in store, just glad to be spared the exhaustion of having to walk in the condition we were in. The 'dugouts' were very narrow and allowed for no movement from us whilst floating which meant remaining in a cramped position but there was no option if we hoped to proceed. Those too ill lay across our laps which meant we were in great discomfort. The current was erratic and very powerful in places so negotiating it called for strong nerves which, of course, we did not possess at this stage. My Grandmother was in near hysteria most of the time and the grown-ups did on occasion have to use firm persuasion to calm her. How she must have suffered - poor dear.

CHAPTER FIFTEEN

"Arrival at Nhkrina Ga Village"

With our two Kachin guides acting as oarsmen, we followed the river, keeping as close to the bank as possible and we prayed that the rain may cease. The rain ceased and the sun shone brightly, at first warming our chilled bodies with its warm rays and then proving to be too strong for our bare heads now void of much hair. My Mother made us cover our heads with any available cloth. Towards late afternoon we noticed that we were in sight of what looked to be a fair sized village. This was the village of Nhkrina Ga where we were pleased to take refuge. We were now nearing the end of June. As we neared this village we noticed the presence of many corpses and people lying outstretched in the mud. We stopped our Canoe to disembark at the sight of a few huts.

On our arrival we found another family there. An Indian Doctor, his wife and two children. Knowing that we had come upon a Doctor was at first reassuring, though we were to soon realise that he was a very sick man and also that without medical supplies there was nothing he could do to help us. They were all sick and weak people. Knowing that the Doctor was suffering from dysentery, my Mother preferred that we not share their hut, so my Uncle bartered yet another "Trading Tool" for the privilege of us occupying a small hut a little distance away. Mr. Bhadu and his family sheltered in another hut nearby.

With Mr. Bhadu acting as interpreter we learned that hundreds of refugees had passed through during the past month. The Doctor and his family were the remnants of a batch of the survivors taking the 102nd mile route. We now knew that at this point our path was nearing the route on which the rest of our family had embarked when we made the decision to travel up to Sumprabum. These people had passed through the valley bypassing Nhkrina Ga and heading for the village of Shingbwiyang at the foot of the Naga Hills. They had hoped to get help to enable them to traverse the Naga Hills before the monsoons had made their exit impossible. Up to this point our little group of 20 had been trekking, from Sumprabum through the mountains, on our own.

Although we were now sheltered from the weather and able to rest in a hut off the rain soaked ground, we were in very poor shape physically but still not willing to give in. We managed to barter some small possession for a little basic food i.e. rice of a coarse variety or a pumpkin.

We had been at this village a couple of days hoping that we could recover our strength somewhat, when my elder brother Victor decided that, with a Kachin for company; he would investigate the possibility of refugees being stranded at the village of Maingkwan. This was not far upstream from the village at which we were resting - though on a different track. The Indian doctor seemed to think that many people were left there, unable to continue, and this made my brother decide to investigate in case he came across any of our family. How he hoped to be able to help them, given his own poor state, is debatable. Nevertheless he felt the need to try.

However, this being the month of June, the strong midday sun beat down on the valley and it seemed that after that first

66

day's walk in it, my brother had suffered severe sunstroke. We were shocked and frightened to see him return the next day, nearly carried by his Kachin companion, delirious and very near death. He raved in this high fever for two whole days and nights and there was so little we could do besides try and keep his brow cool with damp cloths. Those members of the family who were not completely bedridden took it in turn to administer to him. Once again our only medicine being prayer. We were all so relieved to find his fever drop on the third day. Though extremely weak, we could be hopeful that he would survive.

Practically all our 'valued items' of jewellery had by this time been exchanged for the paltry nourishment of a small chicken which was of necessity reserved for the sick rather than the hungry. My use of the term 'valued items' in no way relates to any value other than what it could be exchanged for - to save us!

My Grandmother had by now become exhausted and very weak, her nerves at breaking point. She too had suffered high Malaria fever, stomach upsets, weakness through lack of food and nourishment but her worst suffering was the fear which enveloped her throughout each day and night. Sadly we could find no words to comfort her sufficiently now.

CHAPTER SIXTEEN

"Dysentery Strikes"

We were soon saddened to hear that the Indian Doctor had died from dysentery and a gangrenous leg which resulted from the many leech bites on his leg having turned septic. There was no medication available to prevent this happening and in the days that followed we were to see how this condition spread through so many bodies which lay languishing in the scorching sun.

This was the first death in our vicinity though, even now, my Mother would not permit us to dwell on it, deeply sympathetic though her feelings were. On reflection I realise that she feared that we would recognise the hopelessness of our situation and give up the fight, accepting that death was an inevitable outcome to our plight.

My Grandmother's condition was causing us great anxiety and we were so relieved to have been able to move to a bigger and slightly cleaner hut, some little distance from the one we occupied. We lost no time in making the move, taking with us our paltry few belongings and the Kachins carrying my Grandmother who was unable to walk. That night we thanked God for this unexpected reprieve from the squalor of our previous abode and dared to hope that in our improved surroundings we could all recover a little.

However, it seems that our relief was soon to be shattered by the death of my Grandmother whose tired and frightened mind could no longer fight her bodily ills. She must have suffered a Stroke for she became somewhat paralysed and though conscious to the last, could not communicate with us. We were all with her on the night that God took her and now it seemed that what had happened during the past two months was not just a bad dream! We were now well and truly part of the reality of our fight for survival. For Patsy and myself this was the first family death we had witnessed and as we were particularly attached to my Grandmother, we were entering an unfamiliar depth of suffering.

The date which I clearly remember, was the 1st of July 1942 and it was with broken hearts that we followed her tired but peaceful body to its resting place. The Kachins had agreed to dig a grave as near as to our needs as possible but alas there was no coffin or the like in which to carry out a civilised burial. All we had was a clean woven mat in which to encase her, but I remember how pleased I was at having discovered some pumpkin flowers to place on her grave. In my childish mind I felt that this at least provided a little touch of normality to make up for some of what was missing. Her death dealt us a crushing blow for we still had hoped to survive as a family group. That night we huddled together comforting each other through our tears awaiting dawn and what lay before us with uncertainty, fear and great sadness.

We remained at Nhkrina Ga for another week hoping that this would enable our wounds to heal a bit and our weary limbs be somewhat rested. We were also to have the promise of at least some food. My brother Frank had a leg covered in septic leech bites which were getting worse and this was a source of great anxiety to my Mother and us, especially after the death of the Indian Doctor. Our medical kit was at this stage reduced to a few Aspirins, a couple of bandages, a thermometer and some permanganate of potassium which we used to bathe his leg constantly. As always we prayed because we knew that our treatment fell far short of what was needed to help Frank and we were again begging a miracle.

Although most of us were as yet in no fit state to walk, my Mother and Uncle decided that we move on in our Kachin canoes since we were by now submitting to depression and losing so much of our initial fight. Mr. Bhadu and his family had procured a Canoe for themselves at this village and our family had the two which we arrived in. Both parties were by now sadly reduced in size for besides our loss, Mr. Bhadu had suffered the loss of his two younger children. So it was that with Kachin guides acting as oarsmen, we set off up the Tanai Hka river heading in a north-westerly direction. The widow and children of the Indian Doctor were too weak and ill to leave when we did and we never heard of them again.

Our aim now was to try and reach a village at the end of each day's journey, this being preferable to camping on the river banks. The first village we reached was Taihpa Ga, a village of about the same size as the one we had left.

We found that some of the huts in this village harboured a few sick and dying refugees who had not been able to move on with the main body of trekkers. So many thousands of these poor people were soon to meet their death in this brave attempt. Due to this situation, we were unable to obtain shelter as a family group and for the first time were obliged to split into two groups, sheltering where space was available in these cramped conditions.

The atmosphere of this village was peculiarly indifferent. Although my Uncle had moved around trying to get what information he could concerning the fate of the thousands who had set out from the 102nd mile post, little could be learned. It seemed that many had perished before this stage and many had also carried on, hoping to find help. The few who were in the village were undoubtedly sick in mind and body and seemed content to lie where they were, void of any hope. I remember there being a young couple who seemed more alert than the others, though in poor physical condition and they were so delighted to see us and to know that we still planned to continue with hopes of succeeding. They expressed a desire to join us and although we were in no position to give them any hope, my Uncle did not dissuade them.

CHAPTER SEVENTEEN

"The Mysterious Murder"

After a meagre meal of some rice and a type of wild cabbage we settled ourselves for the night with no encouragement from the groaning forms around us. Mrs. Bhadu and her children found a spot in this hut near us. However, once again my Mother led us in prayer and with this we seemed to find comfort, drifting to a disturbed sleep wondering what the night and next day would bring. Lack of space meant that we were to cling together and support each other avoiding the holes in the mat floor which proved threatening, for so many reasons. I remember being very much afraid on this night because for the first time we were surrounded by strangers in such poor mental and physical condition.

In the dead of night we were startled by the most piercing screams coming from the direction of one of the huts further away from us. We were terrified and clung to each other in fear at the repetition of these piercing cries but we dare not venture out in the darkness to investigate. Patsy and I kept close to my Mother, all thoughts of sleep were abandoned and we once again prayed for the light of dawn.

At daybreak, my Uncle, two brothers and Mr. Bhadu came to our hut, the men having chosen to occupy the hut next to us which was in a worse condition than ours and the occupants more threatening. With the screams coming from the opposite direction they had not thought us to be in danger. However, it was not long before we heard that the young couple, who had wanted to leave with us, had been murdered. In the confusion that followed, I was caught up in a group of horror stricken people bent on confirming these reports and what I witnessed proved a dreadful shock to my impressionable mind, and I refused to leave my Mother's side for days. It was rumoured that this couple had possessed some jewelry which was the motive for their murder – by whom we were not certain. However, we were in no position to investigate at this point.

Understandably, we were more than relieved to leave this village later that day and move on, following the Tanai Hka River, heading for the village of Shingbwiyang which lay at the foot of the Naga Hills. We had realised by now that our troubles were far from over with the Patkai Mountain Range yet to be crossed. This realisation, in the face of our poor physical shape should have all but stripped us of any hope of reaching our goal. Just looking at each other told us so clearly of the dreadful state we were in and should have robbed us of any hope of coming through this ordeal alive. Yet we clung onto our hope of a miracle amidst these horrendous circumstances.

As there were no other villages between us and the village of Shingbwiyang, we were compelled to spend another night on the river bank with the promise of yet more torture from sand flies. We had anchored the canoes just before sunset to give us some daylight in which to set up our shelters and cook a frugal meal of rice and wild yam. Whilst my older sisters were trying to get a fire going and my brothers were putting up the make shift shelter with Mr. Bhadu and the two Kachins, my Uncle was caught up in the excitement of having caught a large fish. Momentarily, our appetites were aroused at the thought of enjoying a little fresh fish. However, our excitement soon turned to horror when we discovered that the form at which my Uncle had fired a shot, turned out to be the much dead and inflated body of a Chinese soldier which had floated downstream to where we were!

CHAPTER EIGHTEEN

"The Chinese Soldiers"

Needless to say this incident somewhat robbed us of our appetite for the frugal meal that followed and kept our thoughts fully occupied during those sunset hours as to what lay in store. The presence of a Chinese soldier in the area worried my Uncle and Mother who sensed that we may have been misguided in our expectation of sanctuary at this village. Although we had reason to be grateful for a dry night, we slept little for we were 'bitten to death' by sand flies - horrendous torture!

Once again we packed our few possessions and set off after no more than a hot drink of Kachin tea to sustain us. About noon that day, when only the sound of the oars striking the water disturbed the silence among and around us, we were shocked by the sudden burst of rifle fire. This was accompanied by the simultaneous disappearance of our Kachin oarsmen into the river.

We were too terrified to move more than our eyes which soon brought into focus the men behind the guns. There, on the opposite bank of the river, were a group of Chinese soldiers, half-naked and some were armed with rifles. Judging by the frightening look on their faces, their intentions were by no means honourable. We had good reason to be afraid of these soldiers who were now making for our canoes. Their dishevelled appearance and look of wild intent struck fear in our hearts. In the few minutes they took to reach us, my eldest sister had, with the rest of us acting as a screen, secured our few most treasured needs in a bundle around her waist, giving each of us some small thing to hide.

When the Chinese soldiers reached us they nearly tipped us all out in their eagerness to 'get at us'. I remember noticing the awful stench of their bodies as they approached us and we were all praying aloud by this time, with our rosary beads firmly entwined in our fingers. They had begun pulling our canoes over to the other bank where the rest of their group waited. It is hard to describe our feelings at this moment but I remember my Mother encouraging us to pray louder and louder which we did!

Once again it seemed that God had not deserted us for the sight of our Rosary beads and the sound of our prayers obviously had some effect on their Captain, who was armed. We assumed him to have been educated in a Christian School in China for, on hearing our prayers; he immediately barked orders at the men which drew them off mumbling. Their attempt was not without some gain for they had impounded our small supply of rice and pumpkins together with two much needed blankets.

The Captain questioned my Uncle as to where we were heading - in broken English, and when my Uncle told him that we were heading for the village of Shingbwiyang, he indicated that 'we not go there'. He emphasised his advice by running his finger across his throat in a motion descriptive of fatality! They then moved off, leaving us to continue our journey with added anxiety. Seeing the Chinese Soldiers move away our two Kachin oarsmen reappeared, having swam some distance further along the shore and no doubt watched the proceedings from there. Luckily Mr. Bhadu's family were further behind and the Chinese marauders had left the river and moved inland after their encounter with us. Thankfully, they were spared our threatening experience. We were to soon come to realise just how many thousands of retreating Chinese troops there were in the Hukawng Valley trying to escape. They were reduced to a low level of behavior through starvation and posed an added threat to our survival. Few survived.

To us this narrow escape was yet another of the many miracles we witnessed during that Trek and it made us feel that, improbable though it seemed at times, our prayers were being heard. We resumed our journey hoping to make the village before dusk. Although our spirits were low and we were filled with anxiety as we approached it, we were in no way prepared for what we encountered on arrival.

We noticed an unfamiliar smell and at about the same time saw bits of floating debris which included body parts. This told us that we were nearer our goal than we had imagined and that conditions there would possibly be horrifying. It was now raining heavily, so we huddled under the cover of the ground sheet, still hoping for the comparative shelter of a hut at this village.

We reached the outskirts of Shingbwiyang in the late evening and to our great concern we noticed several refugees lying on the sand. Some under the pathetic cover of a ragged blanket, others just lying in the mud, with flies swarming all over them.

As the bank rose sharply away from the river, my Uncle, Mr Bhadu and Victor decided to investigate the possibility of shelter for us, suggesting that the rest of us remain in the canoes till they returned. The sickly permeating smell all about us made us sick to our stomachs and for the first time I saw my Mother openly crying, whilst hugging us to her. Having waited in the rain for what seemed an eternity, with still no sign of the men, my Mother decided that we should investigate and so we all got out of the canoes and climbed the muddy slopes which were littered with human debris. It was near dark by this time. Our Kachin 'Oarsmen' had disappeared on arrival sensing the danger of remaining in this cauldron of death and disease.

On reaching the top we were to freeze in our steps at the indescribable squalor that lay before our eyes. At this point the men returned with grim faces only to tell us that it would not be possible to have a hut to ourselves no doubt trying to soften the blow, for we needed no words to describe our present plight. It seemed we had arrived at "Hell on Earth".

CHAPTER NINETEEN

"Shingbwiyang - Hell on Earth"

As we followed my Uncle and Brothers to the hut which we were to shelter in, we had to pick our way in the rain, through the numerous bodies that lay everywhere. People sat around in the rain - small groups, just staring. Others lay in the mud, whining softly as if this brought them some comfort. The squalor covering every step we took made us 'freeze'. We noticed that several forms lay outstretched with eyes glazed and the stench was unbearable although we kept our mouths and noses buried in our small bundle of clothing, crying as we walked.

When my Uncle stopped by one of the huts, we could hardly believe that this was where we were to shelter, for there were outstretched forms both dead and alive everywhere. However, we followed my Uncle and brothers up the steps of this hut wondering where, amidst all this squalor, we were to settle. It was soon evident that with the expulsion of the dead from a corner, we were to clear a space for ourselves! This was an area about eight feet square which meant that we only had enough room to sit huddled together on our blankets. All around us were dead and dying and in these conditions it was impossible to stomach even a drink. The stench and filth surrounding us was surely the end of our hopes for survival. We shivered with shock and fear and it seemed we could no longer fight these odds. Even prayer seemed out of place. Yes - This was surely 'Hell on Earth'. Oh God how could we survive!

My Mother was so overcome by despondency that she cried uncontrollably with us for it seemed too much to hope that we could come out of this alive. It seemed that even God had deserted us now! My Uncle and Brothers set about removing the four bodies left occupying the corner which was to be our shelter, by dropping them out of the exit door of the hut on to the ground below! We tore pieces of our blankets to wet under the pouring rain to wipe the floor which was covered in human excreta and blood. This we continued doing whilst crying - aloud at times - now experiencing for the first time a strong will to die and so not have to suffer in this way any longer. I remember my Mother thanking God that my Grandmother was not with us to endure this terrible suffering.

My beloved Mother once again found reason to lift our hearts a little by pointing out our 'good fortune' in being placed by the exit door of the Hut which meant that we had air to breath - foul as it was - and the rain beating down gave us clean water. We were also able to relieve our bladders without having to make our way through all the human debris in the Hut!

Amidst all the pain and suffering we had endured since leaving Sumbrabum we had not until now been plunged into such an abyss of degradation. That night was to see us 'clawing at life' in trying to find ways to sustain our dignity as human beings. We were all sick to our stomachs and shivered uncontrollably with fever and fear. Our eyes were sore with crying and it seemed that all our hopes were to die here with us. The smells and sounds which filled this hut robbed us of our ability to drink anything other than the rain water which filled our Brown Cooking Pot, laid by the door. Once again coming under the spell of my dear Mother's Faith and Trust in God, we sat huddled together and prayed for the light of dawn and yet another miracle!!

Morning came and with it a more vivid picture of our predicament for we had not been able to see too much in the near darkness of the previous evening. My Uncle and brothers immediately went in search of the two officials – One Government Officer and an Army Major whom we understood to be "in charge" of setting up a half way Camp as it were, for the refugees. We were told they were the existing Authority for helping survivors.

My Uncle was encouraged when he heard this and set out to find them and get what help they could give us to continue our trek. We soon realised how futile were our hopes.

We sat huddled in this squalid hut crying, dispirited, sickened by the stench and horrified by the sights and sounds around us. It seemed that we had obtained this shelter from the rain at a very high premium, for these conditions did more than all the suffering and hardship of the past two and a half months, to weaken our faith and hope. These were of course our only weapons in our fight for survival.

All around us were people barely hanging on to life, having lost control of all bodily functions and crying out in delirium at every moving shadow. It seemed too much to think that we could survive in these surroundings and our hopes were crushed into the mud and filth of this hut. My dear Mother with her great courage tried to find ways of comforting us by concentrating on the possibility of moving to an improved shelter. She called on us to take stock of our paltry possessions!

Our Symbols of Comfort and Hope

These amounted to no more than an odd item of clothing, a few tin plates, mugs, our faithful cooking pot, a Statue of Mary, one of Saint Jude - patron of miracles - and a Crucifix. (Pictured as in my possession today) There was also a treasured bundle of family photographs part of which was soaked by this time and we each had one well worn blanket. I have been able to use a few of the treasured photographs in support of my story. This was the sum total of our worldly goods! In reality it did not matter to us what our possessions were but my dear Mother knew that she needed us to focus on what we had succeeded in doing to get here and so not give up our fight to survive.

We could no longer be protected from the bizarre nature of our surroundings, where we were witnessing life at its lowest. I remember an old man calling out to us for water. He had evidently been lying there for days suffering acute dysentery, covered in flies, which he hadn't the strength to drive off his face and body. The stench surrounding him was unbearable. My Mother did not hesitate to support his poor dirty head on her arm and give him a drink of the rain water which was beating down on us at the time. His sunken eyes looked up at her with gratitude and then closed for the last time, ending his suffering... This took place a few feet from where we were, placing us close to death in more ways than one. What a tribute to my dear Mother's humanitarian strength and a lasting example to us all. Many years later I had need to draw on this strength.

We were to later hear of this Hukawng Valley being referred to as "The Valley of Death" so named due to the massacre of hundreds of Tribes people by Naga Headhunters not so long before our venture into the valley. We were now witnessing the events which gave birth to that reference in our case.

About the middle of the morning my Uncle and brothers returned from their visit to the 'Official Hut' and by the stricken look on their poor unshaven faces we knew that we were to hear bad news. Bad news it was for it seemed that any progress from this 'Camp' was unthinkable due to the rivers being made impassable by the Monsoon rains.

It had also become apparent that the two Officials - one Mr. North who worked for the Burma Frontier Services and a Major Katz were the assumed authority to assist us. It seemed they were more concerned with keeping away from the health dangers that threatened them, instead of helping us, as we had hoped. They were well segregated, in a fenced off Bungalow, away from the huts at this village of Shingbwyang. They had apparently secured provisions for themselves and even had Native Guards on duty - to keep the dying away?

In recalling these sad circumstances I still feel a sense of disgust and betrayal. It could be said that our plight and that of the thousands whose only escape was through these Jungle routes, was the result of much mismanagement by the Government Authorities during the Japanese conquest of Burma.

To this day I carry the memory of my dear Uncle a man of considerable stature, breaking down and crying uncontrollably at this point - I had not witnessed this before and knew that the situation must have been hopeless. He felt that we had been abandoned to the fate of the masses despite our brave fight to reach this village. We had hoped to get the help we needed to proceed and thus survive this perilous Trek but we soon realised that help of this nature was not on offer!

The existence of this 'Camp' became plain to us since these were undoubtedly the thousands of exhausted starving refugees who had arrived too late to beat the swollen rivers and so were trapped in this base camp starving - dangerously ill, perilously weak and without any hope.

Whereas they must have arrived here sick and weak, the primeval conditions in which they had been existing, coupled with the lack of hygiene, had given rise to the spread of the most serious type of dysentery, malaria and other fevers. These diseases together with the many other privations endured, took its toll of the numbers who had reached this Camp. We were surrounded by hundreds of dead and dying. Many people who had reached the point of total mental breakdown. A sea of sadness and suffering. How could we hope to come out of this alive! Witnessing such suffering in such close proximity broke our hearts and filled us with fear. One cannot imagine these conditions, however eloquently described because all of what we were witnessing and enduring went far beyond the extent of ones imagination. What is more, we were very much part of this suffering ourselves.

Some of the Huts housed the remnants of Chinese Soldiers - it seemed there were scores of them in varying stages of wild uncontrolled behaviour. Their aim was to secure food for themselves, not caring about the means used to obtain this. To us they proved dangerous and threatening. My Mother was constantly afraid of their intent with so many girls in our family group. It was with great relief that my Brother Victor came upon a Chinese Army Captain who seemed to still have some authority over the stragglers in his group. This Chinese Captain was to prove a 'friend' over the coming weeks. Through him we obtained two boxes of matches (very precious in our circumstances) and some rice - no doubt part of the store accumulated from the looted Ration Drops!

Whatever our fate was to be, we knew that we could not have survived where we were so my poor Uncle made repeated walks up to Mr. North's hut, trying to prove that we were still willing to fight for our lives and not let our hopes die in this mud and squalor. He could not see my Uncle, it seemed. Too busy - and there wasn't any help he could offer! My Uncle returned crushed by his failure to find a way out for us. About all that could be done by way of satisfying our need for some nourishment that night was to boil a pot of water and using a part of the treasured tin of milk we had been given, made ourselves a hot drink of diluted condensed milk! Once again we were to spend a night of horror in this hut, all of us crying openly staring death in the face but still willing to struggle to reach my Father whom we hoped had arrived safely in India. This was our goal as set out by my Mother and we were to fight to get there.

CHAPTER TWENTY

"Dysentery Strikes Again"

Mr. Bhadu and his family were settled in similar conditions in a hut next to us, and with Mr. Bhadu himself in a high fever, they too seemed to lose hope. His family had suffered further losses by this stage and his wife, no longer with a baby tied to her was, in her weakened state, struggling to comfort her other young ones. My dear Mother gave her a reassuring hug whenever she could and comforted her young ones too.

By the next morning, my Uncle discovered that he had fallen prey to the dreaded dysentery germ and knowing what this could mean, he made a last painful effort to do something to move us from those surroundings which would surely have become our grave. So yet again he approached Mr North for help and all he was given was 'permission' to move to another hut, a little distance from the one we were in, provided that we ourselves were willing to make it habitable. As anything was preferable to our present conditions, my Uncle had accepted the proposition and we were to move right away.

Sadly we noticed that my Uncle was already succumbing to the debilitating effects of this chronic illness and he was barely able to walk with us as we made our way, through all the human debris, to the other hut. As we passed, we heard pitiful cries for help, others crying out in delirium, Mothers clinging to their dead infants, obviously victims of complete mental collapse. What hope could we offer these people when we ourselves were in such a hopeless state. We must have looked emaciated and frail - the only difference as far as I can remember between ourselves and those lying around on the ground - was that we had not yet accepted that we too were about to die!

When we reached the hut, we realised that in this instance the word vacant only meant that none of the occupants were alive! I shall never forget the stench of decomposing flesh which filled the air. A smell which was to haunt us for months to come. Whereas the bodies which had to be removed by us in the first hut had not long been dead, the corpses we were now called upon to remove had obviously been dead for quite a while!

However, my Mother once again rallied us to make a supreme effort in clearing this hut and with little or no energy, we started removing the 'debris'. I remember being horrified to find that when trying to remove one of the bodies with my brother Victor, the limbs came away in our hands! We were all sick to our stomachs during the whole procedure and we girls were shaking with fear. On reflection how could I have at the tender age of 12 coped with this horror! Unimaginable in normal circumstances but, at this point, we had reached a stage of suffering for survival, which bore no likeness to reality. We were in a survival zone where all things normal did not exist. As yet death was somehow not an option for us and so we fought on!

My Mother kept reminding us that soon we would have a hut to ourselves and that then everything would be 'alright'. The power of her assurance must have been strong because we reacted by continuing with our gruesome task in floods of tears. The girls fetched water from the river to wash down the floor and my brothers collected branches with which to patch the roof and the only two walls to the hut. Were we in reality carrying out this horrendous task - only half aware of our surroundings? No - we were unaware of the depths of our suffering - merely going forward to not die - that is all!

A Chinese soldier had befriended us and was of great assistance in helping us clear and patch this hut for ourselves. He was to remain with our family and was known to us as John. We relied on his physical help and good natured support during the dark days that followed, and thankfully he was strong and able enough. Another miracle at the 11th hour it seemed. He was to be of great help to us at this stage.

Throughout this operation, my Uncle Jim had been unable to do more than direct us from the blanket on which he was lying, obviously in great pain. Our first concern was to settle him in the hut and we were not to know that the steps he took into our new shelter were to be his last. In the days that followed he suffered the intense agony of the dysentery which he had contracted at that first hut, and the Malaria fever which afflicted us all.

My dear Mother nursed him constantly, doing everything possible to make him as comfortable as possible but with no medicine, little could be done other than try and comfort him in his agony. We had barely any opium left, so relief was very temporary for him. He continually cried out his regrets at leading us into this 'hell' but my Mother was always quick to reassure him that we owed our lives to his care and leadership.

He was a truly loving, caring man whose deep concern was for his Mother- my Grandmother - who had died earlier, my Mother - his sister to whom he was devoted and us - his family too - because he had no children of his own. His lovely Shan wife whom he loved dearly had chosen to remain in a village across the water from Myitkyina with her family.

Patsy, Uncle Jim & me - 1941

My Mother knew the great risk she was running in nursing him and for this reason would not allow us too near, tending to all the details of his needs herself. At the same time she tried to establish a routine of some sort, to give us the incentive to continue fighting for our lives. We feared so much for our beloved Mother but knew that she could do no other than be there for my poor Uncle who had done everything he could to ensure our survival.

We had to go down to the river to wash whenever able to. It also meant washing with sand as soap when our small supply ran out. This meant picking our way through squalor but we needed to reach upstream where the river would be cleaner. Our clothing was washed as often as one or two of us were able to manage. This also had to be done upstream so that the water not be contaminated by the many bodies floating around, and the unbelievable filth surrounding the refugees still camped in squalor on the banks.

One of these washing expeditions proved disastrous for my dear sister Phyllis, who amidst her many ills, had, with Gloria, kept our domestic needs going as best they could. She had on this particular day taken with her all of the few items of clothing we had to change into, meaning to freshen them by a dip in the stream. Sadly she was to return in tears, minus the clothes for it seemed the current had played tricks on her and carried the lot away!

We were now reduced to just the clothing we stood in but with our sheer determination to retain some degree of human pride, I soon fashioned for us a change of clothing out of our "findings" amongst the debris. An inherited 'talent' which came in useful at this critical time. I recall removing clothing from Corpses in Military Uniform and washing and using this to fashion some form of dress for Patsy and myself! Whereas the thought of this makes me now shudder, our environment and necessity at the time were such that survival was our only concern and our means of achieving it were of little importance. My Sister Joyce's small bundle containing thread and needles proved invaluable at this juncture.

CHAPTER TWENTY ONE
"The Ration Drop"

It seemed that the Army Authorities in India were aware of the existence of this camp and had started making attempts to drop food to us. At first, much of this food was lost, since the nature of the Country with its jungle clad hills made low flying impossible. Weather conditions also hampered the success of these 'drops'. Besides, there were many starving desperate people including stragglers from the Chinese army - willing to kill for the gain of even a little food. We were to witness some bizarre human behaviour brought on by starvation and desperate need. There were also dangers to be faced, with the uncertain destiny of these heavy sacks dropping from such a height with no specific marked dropping zone. These sacks consisted of coarse rice with an enclosed large tin of corned beef.

The "drops" were to be collected and taken to Mr North's godown where it was supposedly 'distributed' to the starving remains of human beings. Some well past benefitting and others like us suffering from all manner of illness which made even the taking of meagre food offerings beyond us.

However, to have any food at all by this stage was a miracle to us and we did our best to extract some sustenance from whatever was allotted.

Of our little group, Gloria seemed to remain the strongest not having yet been afflicted by the diarrhoea or malaria which was taking its toll of us all at this time. She alone kept us sipping tea and anything else she could concoct with the meagre rations available. We were all falling prey to fever and weakness – our limbs too sore to rely on.

It did however mean that we were now having to subsist on a diet of some grain (I remember Rice and Lentils of a greenish variety) and tinned Corn Beef. These rations though insufficient for normal needs did afford us some food and sparingly carried us through from one food drop to another. The monsoons made it impossible to predict the regularity of such 'Food Drops'.

It was now, on one of these dropping missions, that I was to narrowly miss being killed. There I was sitting in front of the mud enclosed fire, encouraging the flames so that our pot of water soon boil for our longed for cup of Kachin tea. We had through sheer necessity got to accept the taste of this, though it was more the comfort of the warmth it brought to our chilled bodies that made it inviting. I was so pleased, as we all were, to hear the drone of aircraft, which was our one sign of hope in these dark days, for it meant the promise of food and possibly some medicine.

The next thing I remember was lying by my mother with an aching head and neck and very sore hands. Apparently my Mother was grief stricken thinking that I had died. One of the bags of grain, containing a 15 pound tin of Corned Beef had come straight through our frail make shift roof, landing near where I was sitting having thrown me forward onto the fire. By some miracle, the water had extinguished the fire, so the burns on my hands were not as severe as they could have been. My poor mother and family had been so worried on my account because I had been knocked unconscious, suffering a severe concussion no doubt. On reflection the nature of the accident should surely have killed me. We were witnessing yet another miracle!

However, after many worrying hours for my family I regained consciousness and my crying was apparently enough sign of me being alive and there was hope that I would recover! My head was very sore and I was somewhat hazy in my perception for quite a while after this, but I appeared to have miraculously escaped death or at least more severe injury. Yet another miracle just when we seemed to have run out of them! For many years I suffered severe headaches which could have been a result of this life threatening incident. Not surprisingly I could not bear to smell or eat Corned Beef for a very long time after the Trek associating this with our 'nightmare'!

My poor Uncle died on the 1st of August 1942, having suffered a great deal and although it was a terrible blow to us, we felt consolation in the thought that his suffering had come to an end. My Mother was broken hearted and fearful for the fate of us all. Once again we could only manage the minimum of burial rites, having had to bury him wrapped in the blanket on which he had suffered so much. My brothers and the Chinese boy dug a shallow grave near our hut and my Uncle was buried there with all of us present, a lost band of broken hearted souls weak in body and spirit. My brother merely 'troubled' Mr North for a death certificate – that was all! We chose to put him to rest ourselves – our love, thanks and prayers being his casket.

With the death of my Uncle, who had undoubtedly been the physical leader and strength of our party we had suffered an immeasurable loss and our hopes of survival were further reduced. However once again my Mother, despite her sadness and with her seemingly unbreakable faith and great courage rallied our spirits by convincing us that having gone through so much we were not going to be beaten now. She always showed us a way to find hope even in the midst of hopeless circumstances! Her faith and courage were so powerful! I realized that I myself dipped into this gift of hers later in my own life.

So we continued our fight against the surrounding horrors and the fevers that one or other of us were continually afflicted with. My eldest sister Joyce had been suffering the crippling pain of rheumatism in both legs brought on no doubt by having sat through that night on the riverbank with her legs soaking in pools of water. She had remained in a cramped position, whilst she sheltered my mother and sister Patsy who were both delirious with a high fever at the time. Now she could not walk with the pain in her legs and this was for us an added anxiety.

By now, most of the thousands of refugees had died not being able to fight these terrifying odds. The Officials had organised help in partly clearing the area of the countless dead - mostly dumping the remains in the surrounding jungle - which meant that we were continually surrounded by the awful stench of decomposing bodies. A few people remained in the village hanging on to life, some with little or no purpose it seemed. In truth what purpose could anyone hang on to in these circumstances? Very few were to survive long enough to attempt the next stage of this dreadful trek – over the Kumon Range to Assam.

CHAPTER TWENTY TWO

"Our Leading Light Fades"

It was now, to our horror, that we found my dear Mother had also become a victim of the killer dysentery germ and this realisation filled us with a fear that we had not felt before. We prayed desperately and suffered agonies of mind and body watching her condition deteriorate from day to day. Knowing this, my brother Frank decided that, with Victor and Joyce to keep us going, he and the Chinese boy would attempt to get through somehow, in order that help be obtained to save my Mother. They were to attempt another precarious route known to the Kachin guide who agreed to lead Frank and our Chinese friend John through to Assam. He felt compelled to try anything in our attempt to save her.

He knew that without help even her truly brave determination and faith would not suffice, so in spite of her desperate pleas, he bade us a quick farewell and set off towards the Naga Hills, with his Chinese companion. All the supplies they carried was a blanket each and a small supply of our rations, not knowing the route or anything of the nature of the hills which they were to cross and, above all, with just one native guide. The Officials had also warned against such an attempt because the rivers were not yet regarded as passable. However, the fear of my Mother dying must have given my brother the necessary courage for nothing could make him change his mind. He balanced the odds and concluded that the risk he was taking was not much different to our chance of survival.

When we said good-bye to him, we felt sure that we would never see him again and my Mother was greatly distressed at his departure on such a hopeless mission, especially in such poor physical condition. Now there was just my Mother, Sisters Joyce, Phyllis, and Patsy, my Brother Victor, Gloria and myself. With my Mother so ill, Victor and Joyce shared the responsibility of making decisions although my poor Mother tried hard to hide her condition from us, lest we lose faith. Thankfully, by this time Joyce's legs were a little stronger and she was able to move a little.

A few days after Frank had left with his companion, Gloria decided that as she still had enough physical strength she would attempt to trek to India via a different route to the one which my brother had taken. This on hearsay from others. By this time rumours abounded of possible exit routes from this Valley. None, of course, tried and tested. This route was to follow a Naga trail which lead from village to village but which entailed the crossing of very steep mountain passes. She felt that with a Naga to guide her she would prefer to attempt this rather than chance crossing the flooded rivers on the route which my brother Frank and his companion had taken. So she left us with her small supply of food and a blanket, seemingly very optimistic. We did not blame her for leaving because we knew that to remain where we were meant accepting that the odds of her survival were very small.

We were all sorry to see her go for we did not share her optimism and besides she had become very dear to us and we depended on her help so much, she being the most able bodied member of our family group. However, two days later we were overjoyed to have her return, having found the going too rough and I suspect that she also felt the loneliness of her plight amidst the danger too much to carry on. There was certainly a happy reunion that day.

It was at this point that an Airdrop had brought a package addressed to my Mother and when it eventually came into our possession you can imagine our reaction. It was a little parcel from my Father containing a letter to my Mother and small amounts of various items of medicinal need including 3 packets of Essence of Chicken, Glucose, Aspirin, Horlicks Tablets, Chocolate and Antiseptic Cream. Even as I write this account I cannot fully convey the feelings we shared at this time. My Mother read the letter to us, eyes full of tears as were ours, - and kept saying "God has answered our prayers - your Daddy is safe". This was my Mothers continual aim for our survival throughout this horrendous Trek. However, she was well aware that when we left our home in Syriam my Father had to remain at his post to be part of the demolition crew of the Burmah Oil Company ensuring that the refined oil reserved was not available to the advancing Japanese army. Their survival and journey to Calcutta was fraught with danger. My Father's fate was not known to us when we set out on the Trek hence this letter brought so much solace to our hearts answering my dear Mothers prayer and confirming her determination that we continue to fight to reach him. The letter also brought her the very special news she had always prayed for - that my Father had been Baptised in our Faith which she so loved and wanted to share with him.

It seemed that my Father had been anxiously awaiting news, travelling to all the points on the Border with India to get news of us. He was a very distraught man who had contacted Military Authorities continually during those difficult months. They had suggested that now that 'Air Drops' were taking place in the Hukawng Valley, my Father should refer to the Authorities to see whether he could make contact with us - that is if we were still alive! This my Father did and it was surely by yet another miracle that the parcel arrived at the Camp just a few days before my beloved Mother died. As far as I am aware no other communication of this nature was ever received on the Trek, in this way.

About this time an Army Doctor had been dropped by parachute to render assistance but tragically it seemed that for us he had arrived too late for my Mother's condition was by this time critical. He had a small supply of medicines with him and although he lost no time in doing what he could for her, it seemed that to hope for a cure at this stage was asking for another miracle but we did. We prayed as we had never prayed before and also having to hide our tears from my Mother who would not have wanted us to give up. This Army Doctor was to be remembered with gratitude for his kindness and spiritual comfort in these very dark days.

However, though his limited medical supplies prevented him from effecting miraculous cures, he gave us all the help he could. He was responsible for arranging that we move to a bigger and cleaner hut and we were greatly heartened by the improvement in our surroundings.

It didn't take us long to move our few belongings and, with my brother carrying my Mother, we walked the fifty yards or so to our new abode. Whereas we were spared the horrendous clearing we had been obliged to carry out at that first hut, we nevertheless had to wash the bamboo floor down and discard any refuse left by the previous occupants. They had obviously left to attempt to trek on, despite the danger of impassable rivers and we were unsure as to whether they were among the hundreds of brave desperate people who perished in the latter stages. We were pleased to settle ourselves in these improved surroundings, each choosing a spot to arrange our 'Mattresses' which were washed Hessian bags and our 'pillows' which were our Bundles containing our change of clothes. Our 'Cover' was our one and only Blanket each, which had been subjected to rough jungle use and which was by this stage threadbare in several places.

We hurriedly got a clean spot organised on which my Mother could lie and when we had settled her found to our great joy that she was brighter and apparently feeling better. We were filled with hope and relished the thought of yet another miracle. As it was my Mother's birthday, 16th September 1942, we were enjoying the special treat of "homemade bread" which Gloria had achieved through steaming a form of dough. It was the first 'meal' we had enjoyed for, besides the luxury of something 'special' to eat, the fact that my Mother was joining us, seemingly on the road to recovery, made it a fitting 'birthday celebration'.

The thousands of refugees in this Camp had by now been reduced to but a few, the majority having died. There were rumours that the Camp Officials were considering a possible date for survivors to be given some assistance to continue the Trek through the Naga Hills. I recall a handful of those remaining did attempt to resume the Trek hoping that the rivers would now be passable. It was now the 16th of September and we felt that we too may be able to move on very soon, if my Mother's condition allowed. Now that she seemed so much better, our hopes ran high.

I remember awaking the following morning with an unfamiliar warmth of feeling. On collecting my thoughts I remembered that it was because my Mother was getting better and we were soon going to be able to move on towards our goal!

In a matter of hours our whole world was to completely collapse for, by the middle of that morning, we realised that my Mother had suffered a relapse and was once again in the agony she had suffered these past weeks. We could find no consolation now for, however much she tried to comfort us, we knew that she would possibly never now recover. Her constitution had been so weakened by the past four months of horror and the dysentery and fevers she was suffering.

We cried, we prayed, we hoped and we despaired in turn. To my mind all was lost for, to carry on without her seemed impossible and undesirable. My older sisters and brother tried to comfort us younger ones and the Doctor was a frequent visitor doing what he could to ease my Mother's pain. He was to give us much needed moral support at this very difficult time.

Eventually, partly from the effects of exhaustion and partly from the effects of the drug injected into her, she slipped quietly into a deep sleep. She lay in this sleep for the next two days during which we could do nothing other than sit by her side and pray, as only she had taught us how. We were expert miracle searchers by this time and our prayers wavered between pleas and demands. As I write I realise that God understood 'where we were at' if our behaviour was irreverent at times like this. Our souls cried out for help because the thought of losing someone as special as my Mother was unbearable to us.

Gloria, though nearly as broken hearted as we were, carried on doing what was necessary, insisting that we eat and drink a little. Finally, on the 19th of September, my dear Mother came out of this sleep and in a voice, seemingly freed of pain, called us to her and made us promise that we would continue fighting to survive and reach my Father. She spoke of a beautiful place awaiting her with a lot of children in her view! This will probably be regarded as hallucination by unbelievers but we took comfort from associating this vision with her life of loving and caring for so many needy children. Saying this she closed her eyes and, with a serene expression long since absent from her dear face, she went to her rest.

I still find it impossible to find words to describe our feelings at her loss for besides having lost our nearest and dearest we were like a small craft in the Ocean, caught in a storm, now without our Captain and guide. It seemed that without her no 'Port' was worth entering! All I can remember at this stage was my horror at having to bury her as we had been compelled to bury my Grandmother and Uncle. That night was one of intense loss and fear for all of us. I only wanted to be with her; life no longer seemed worth fighting for. My family told me that I lost my will and strength completely and for the next three or four days took no food nor did I participate in any conversation, seemingly unwilling to fight. They were deeply troubled and did all they could to revive my will to live which up to this point had been so strong for my age. However, I feel that my dear Mother's influence must have made me regain my concern for the rest of my family and my will to survive returned.

CHAPTER TWENTY THREE

"Our Greatest Loss'"

The Doctor had come forward with whatever consolation and help he could give and promised to conduct as worthy a burial as possible in these conditions. So it was that on the following morning we laid my Mother to rest, wrapped in our best blanket and with a newly woven mat, obtained from the Kachins in exchange for some rations, as her casket.

Our little group, so heartbroken and lost without our chief comforter and inspiration, followed in procession as we made our way towards the shallow grave which had been dug, next to the spot where my Uncle was buried. The doctor said some prayers and we followed as best we could but our voices were too muffled by sorrow to echo far. What could we pray for now, except that my Mother be rewarded for being the loving and exceptional person she was. I remember my sister Joyce trying to comfort Patsy and me as we sadly made our way back to the hut. My one thought at that moment was to wish that I too could have died with my Mother, for the thought of continuing without her was unimaginable and undesirable. I remember returning to her grave time and time again and not wanting to leave it but my dear Brother Victor, who was himself very close to my Mother, and who must also have been suffering deeply, gently lifting me up and carrying me back to our Hut. Our little group were suffering as never before.

My family later told me that during the next few days I had gone into a sort of 'mental freeze', not knowing or caring what happened around me. They had forced me to drink a little, being most anxious as to whether the loss of my will would mean a physical collapse as well. After a few days I had apparently began to gradually recover, receiving all the comfort and encouragement my brother and sisters could give me. They were so pleased to be able to surprise me with a 'new dress', as a few items of clothing had been included in a recent drop. Gloria did her best to encourage my appetite by producing variations on our meagre rations and my family were happy to have me gradually 'return to them', even if only in part.

The weeks following were in many ways the hardest to bear. Fevers and broken sores on our feet made the prospect of walking again unthinkable but we knew we had to overcome this and press on if we were not to die. Bandages (made out of torn strips of cloth washed in rain water) were much in demand! We had to attempt the second half of our journey knowing that we were fast losing so much of our former determination. The last two months at this Camp had left us weak in body and spirits - our limbs having become stiff from lack of exercise after having strained them to the point of exhaustion to get here. All that we had endured sapped us of our physical and moral strength. Above all we were without our "Inspiration and Hope" and we missed her strength of spirit so much.

Within the next two weeks a small group of survivors left the village with Naga bearers to carry those unable to walk and some degree of food supplies for the rest of the Trek. They were hoping to succeed now that the Monsoons were expected to have lessened in intensity enabling the crossing of the fast flowing Rivers ahead.

There were now only our group of survivors left and we knew that we would need to move on before we became too frail to cope with the traumas which awaited us. Our feet were slightly improved and we had found ways to apply bandages as part protection. We were now hoping that we would soon be able to attempt the second challenge to our survival and leave this Cauldron of Death.

Our group now included two girls about the same ages as my sister Patsy and myself. These children had seen the rest of their family die and were themselves in very poor shape, especially the older girl who was unable to walk. My Sister Joyce was not too keen to assume the responsibility of attempting to take them through to safety, since we had no idea just what lay ahead of us, once we had left this Camp. However, as we were amongst the few refugees planning to leave with any hope of succeeding, we were asked to take them with us - which we did.

Mr. Bhadu and two of his older children, if I remember correctly, were the only survivors of his family and they had set out from Shingbwiyang a few weeks or so before we did. We did not meet up with them again, nor hear any news concerning their eventual fate, so hoped that they had made it through to safety.

So it was that in the second week of October we decided to resume our Trek, having partially recovered from our many severe medical problems. We packed our few belongings and got ready to move on but not before paying a farewell visit to my Mother's and Uncle's graves. Broken hearted though we were, we seemed to gain fresh courage from that sad visit and I think it is true to say that, the sight of those two Crosses in that mud covered clearing, was significant of our near lone faith in a sea of despair and desolation!

It was now the third week of October, in the late morning, on a day made exceptional by the absence of rain and bright sunshine that we set out from Shingbwiyang to face the Naga Hills. As we made for the jungles we were soon aware of the challenge ahead of us. We were now to cross the 4000ft Patkoi Mountain Range with all the jungle torments of our previous Trek through the Kumon Range. Whereas we were previously helped by Kachin Guides we were now in Naga territory using two Naga Bearers. Although we were aware of our need to resume Trekking in order to reach our goal, we were now sadly without our "Leaders" whose strength and guidance we had relied on so much. We were also weakened further by our stay in Shingbwiyang with all its horrors and sufferings.

We carried with us a small supply of food, a blanket each, our ground sheets, faithful cooking pot, enamel plates and mugs, and our few 'Treasures'. We also carried a much prized change of clothing. One guide was able to carry most of these supplies whilst the other carried the older of the two children who had joined our little group. She was the weakest among us although by this stage many of us were beyond coping with what lay ahead.

The going was rough from the start and I must have been just about on the last reserve of strength because I remember my brother Victor having to fashion for me a walking stick, from a sturdy bit of branch, to use as an 'aid' in climbing the hills. I hadn't gone very far when I had the overwhelming desire to return to that graveside where my heart was still very much attached. In trying to retrace my steps I was quickly stopped by my sister Joyce. She saw the need to force me to keep going in spite of my distress and I realise now that this must have been at the cost of her own emotions. She, with my Brother Victor, took on the full responsibility of our pledge to our Mother and we owe them our undying gratitude for the way in which they led us through those latter stages of the Trek.

Our stiff limbs, weakened bodies and heavy hearts did nothing to quicken our pace besides the fact that having not walked for the past two months, our feet found the paths we trod, cruelly hard. We were now in the Patkoi foothills with the unenviable need to once again traverse another huge Mountain Range. The paths were steep and with the now diminishing monsoon rains still blighting our progress, they were slippery and dangerous - so much a pattern of those earlier months of trekking through the Kachin hills.

Very soon we came upon the skeletons of hundreds of people who had obviously tried to beat the monsoon flooded rivers but, for obvious reasons, had not made it. Numerous huts, crudely set up, still partially sheltered the remains of little groups of those brave hearted people who had undoubtedly hoped to reach safety, just as we were now hoping to. Skeletons were visible everywhere. After the sights we had witnessed at Shingbwiyang, we were past being horrified and had long since accepted death as a logical possibility although never willing to surrender our will to live.

We followed much the same pattern as our earlier Trek over the Kachin Hills trying to cover as much ground as possible, continuously fighting the terrors and torments of the jungle. Somehow it all seemed so much worse now, for we were so few and of course, so much weaker. We had lost our leader and our **'guiding light'** so it was now so hard to believe in the impossible!

Within a day or two of climbing we looked back on a piece of cleared land at the foothills by which ran a stream and my Brother Victor pointed it out to us - "Look down there - that is - Shingbwiyang" was all he said. We just looked at each other; hugged and cried our farewells to our loved ones now buried there.

Many years later we were to learn that General Stilwell's Army had carried out their re-entry Road to Burma via the Hills and Valley through Shingbwiyang. This thought caused us much heartbreak at the time, knowing that this was the graveyard where our loved ones were left to rest. Only our faith in knowing they were in God's safekeeping gave us the comfort we needed.

About a week's Trek from Shingbwiyang, we came upon what appeared to be a larger than usual group of ragged remnants of huts and skeletons. Since we were obliged to camp at this spot for the night, we wandered around 'investigating'. To our sorrow, we discovered that one of these makeshift huts housed the remains of my Uncle Arthur, his wife and two children. We had parted from them when they chose to Trek by the 102nd mile route and we chose to make for the village of Sumprabum early in May 1942.

At Shingbwiyang we had been told by one of the refugees, who had since died, that she had seen my Uncle and his family together with my other Aunt and her two children, setting out from the village. They were apparently in poor shape but desperate to make it before the monsoons had made the rivers impassable and knowing this, we had been constantly on the look-out for any clues concerning them.

My Uncle Arthur's children - Conrad, Alan and Camille

There was little doubt that the remains that we had now come upon were those of my Uncle Arthur and his family for, besides the fact that the largest frame bore the unmistakably prominent forehead of my Uncle, there was his Police Briefcase, containing papers of identification. Sodden but familiar items of clothing were in evidence. We noticed the absence of the fifth skeleton which would have appropriately conformed to the size of my eldest cousin and assumed that he alone of the family, had carried on. As I write this I wonder how I could have at that age been so perceptive and accepting of the horrific nature of things, as to commend it to my memory as being a logical sequence to our lives at the time.

Having to accept such horror in no way reduced the sadness we felt in these circumstances. Tears flowed and it was hard to carry on our fight to survive. A feeling of hopelessness was now our constant companion!

We were, of course, also looking for evidence of my brother Frank and his companion having passed through but as they had barely any possessions with them, there would have been no trail in this way. Not to have found him dead on the way, was in itself some comfort, though we feared that he may have taken the wrong path, there being several instances when the Nagas would choose one of two paths.

Once again we struggled up high mountain slopes, covered in wet undergrowth, with all the familiar hazards of the first stage. The rivers were in many instances more hazardous and with our party so sadly reduced in size, the effort of struggling against the current, sapped us of the little energy we had left. We would be compelled to rest after such an effort and in this way progress was slow.

CHAPTER TWENTY FOUR

"Patsy is Lost"

My sister Patsy who was now too weak to walk was once again being carried by a Naga guide, this being possible because our supplies were now reduced and we were able to share the load of the little that remained amongst us. Strictly speaking I was not able to take on much of a share since it was all I could do to keep walking, with the aid of a support stick fashioned by my ever caring Brother Victor, with only a small bundle tied to my back.

It was at this stage that we had the frightening experience of having "lost" Patsy. The Naga who was carrying her seemed bent on keeping ahead of the group however much we protested but he had never been out of calling range. As we were accustomed to doing, we had stopped for a rest about noon, when we usually had a little to drink or eat - not much - just enough to give us the strength to keep going.

We noticed that in spite of the calls of the other Naga bearer who was with us (he had been carrying the weaker of the two sisters who had joined our little group at Shingbwiyang) there was no answering call and no Patsy in sight. We waited a few minutes and then started calling her name in all directions. Our anxiety was increased by the fact that at this point of the trail, as had often been the case, there were two paths and we had no idea which path he had taken. We decided to split up in two groups and follow each path through the jungle calling to her and then return to our starting point.

This we did several times without success and by now we were crying with fear for her safety. Our search was made all the more difficult by the shrieks of the monkeys and other occupants of the jungle drowning our calls. As the Naga who was carrying Patsy appeared more unfriendly than the others we encountered, this only added to our worry. No doubt our great concern manufactured possible causes for anxiety.

However, in this jungle in which we were exposed to all the previous torments there was nothing else we could do but carry on following the other Naga from whom we had tried to get some idea as to where his friend could be. All we got from him was a shrug of his shoulders and a grin which we were not sure how to interpret. As we walked we cried - our cries being drowned once again by the 'screams' of the jungle.

To our great joy, as we started up the next slope we heard this faint cry, amidst the chattering of monkeys and on looking up saw Patsy still tied to the back of the Naga, on one of the tree branches. Up to now she had been too frightened to cry out but seeing us she began to sob and our own cries too had been turned to those of relief at seeing her unharmed. She was nevertheless in a dreadful state suffering in so many ways poor darling. It seemed that the Naga had merely chosen this as a resting spot till our group caught up with him and he seemed quite bewildered by our show of emotion!

CHAPTER TWENTY FIVE

"The Hornet's nest"

A further two-week's walking distance in dense jungle, climbing high hills, we reached a Naga village which filled us with relief. It was the village of Tagap Ga which appeared nicely set out with green slopes as a back drop but we soon realised that it too had been the grave of so many hundreds of hapless refugees. They had, like us, fought so hard to beat the odds and reach safety but had succumbed to the ravages of this deadly Trek. We were relieved to have reached a point where we could get some food because the small supply we had set out with was by now depleted.

We were not treated in a hostile manner at this village though we had no means of conversing with these Naga people, other than by sign language. We had nothing left to barter, so we could only depend on their generosity in giving us a little food. About this time, it became apparent that my brother Victor was becoming seriously ill, though he struggled on trying to make little of his condition and suffering.

A particularly painful incident which took place at this stage of the Trek, was my uncomfortable acquaintance with hornets. One day, feeling too weary to walk any further, protesting to my family that even if they had to walk on without me, I just had to sit down and rest where I was, I did just that, with painful consequences! I had, of course,

unwittingly sat on a hornets nest. My screams brought the other members of our group quickly to my aid but by this time I had been stung in more places than I care to remember and the agony was unbearable.

Our Naga guides soon produced their natural antidote for such an emergency in the form of specially picked leaves which I was to rub into the affected areas. My sisters and Gloria did this in the midst of my writhing and screaming. Relief did come later but this episode had cost us about two hours walking time and meant that we would have to spend another night amidst the screams of the jungles not being able to make the next village before sunset. So we had to once again bed down in the jungle with all its threatening features. I was in a poor state and longed to have the comfort of my Mother's arms.

Monkeys were everywhere and their shrill call coupled with the screaming birds haunted us now and for months to come. These sounds brought back so many memories of those previous days when we had our Mother to comfort us and make everything seem all right as only she could. Her absence was felt so badly but my Sister Joyce continued to use my Mother's wish as our beacon and urged us to fight on and so it was that we carried on walking.

At the next village, we were shown into a hut in which there were the remains of a few refugees, who had come this far and we were to discover that it was in this village that my other Aunt and her two little girls had perished. Personal items enabled us to make these identifications. They had obviously died some while before. This saddened us deeply because we knew how bravely they must have fought to reach here. Patsy and I recalled having enjoyed so many happy times in the past, playing games with these cousins of ours. Death seemed to have robbed us of so much! That night we lay down to sleep crying our hearts out. We left this village so dispirited and our steps became so much heavier.

We had now reached a stretch of swampland, through which it was nearly impossible to walk. Each step took us deeper into bog and the very effort, of removing each bare foot from the depth to which it had sunk, exhausted us. Our feet were still so sore. We were very much afraid, especially since we were by now trying to support my brother Victor who was becoming weaker each day. He was in a high fever and we knew that his condition was worsening. Having no spare guides, my brother struggled on giving way to the needs of the two girls.

Leeches abounded in this area and we were once again faced with the painful task of removing them from our bodies. There was also evidence of wild animals in the surrounding hills so we were to be more alert which, at this stage, we found very difficult.

It is hard to imagine just how mechanical our steps had become for we were but skin and bone with little or no physical strength. It was as if we were pressed to go on by a will other than our own and I remember often begging my sister Joyce to leave me to die for I was too tired to go on! All the courage I had shown during the first part of our Trek appeared to have been buried with the loss of my Mother. I recall my Sister encouraging me by reminding me that my Brother Victor needed me and so 'I resumed charge' of my determination to survive! I was also taking care of Patsy as I had always done and was to continue to do throughout our lives.

CHAPTER TWENTY SIX

"Help at Hand"

In spite of our low moral at this time, we had retained some sense of humour - humour of a bizarre nature if anything, for I remember hiding behind a tree waiting to frighten Patsy with a Skull I had picked up! On reflection why would Patsy have been 'frightened' by this, bearing in mind how much horror we had come to accept as part of our struggle! I also remember examining the skeletons for signs of something which could prove useful to us. We thought nothing of claiming an item of clothing from these remains if we could have used it for ourselves. We even tried fitting our feet into "Dead men's boots" but the rain had hardened them beyond use to us so we had to continue trekking these jungles in the improvised canvas shoes we were given from one of the Air Drops at Shingbwiyang. I realise that by now our minds were being well and truly 'scrambled' being called upon to retain our dignity, compassion and determination, whilst having to accept degradation and inhuman surroundings as the norm. How could we have within this very short space of time adjusted our expectations of life - to this day this remains an unanswered question!

We were now climbing mountains in the Patkoi Range six to seven thousand feet high. The going was very rough and we had so little to offer by way of physical strength. Whereas our struggle amidst the Kumon Range had proved much the same challenge, we were now in so many ways unsure of our ability to take this on. We had lost our main 'strength and courage source' not having our Uncle Jim and our beloved Mother with us now. Undoubtedly our heavy hearts did nothing to fuel our weary limbs and even the comparative proximity of our journey's end could not make up for the void within our souls. It was at this point that our need to help each other survive, surfaced most and this, I am sure, kept us going. My Brother Victor's condition was deteriorating and we were very sad and concerned. We desperately needed my Mother's assurance and felt her absence continually.

We had now reached the Summit of a Mountain - at the Pangsau Pass - which marked the border between Burma and India. Sometime later, this was to be the route constructed under General Stilwell's Command for Military purposes. It was the building of a 'Road' from Assam through the Hills and Jungles to reach Myitkyina in Northern Burma. They found the nature of the country so horrendous that they nicknamed this Pass "Hell Pass". Steep gradients, hairpin bends, sheer drops of nearly 200 feet and surrounded by thick rain "forests" was how this section was to be described by the Army.

Traversing these high Mountain paths with all the ever present dangers and difficulties took its toll of our will and small reserve of strength. We struggled so much to cover a little ground given the nature of our bodily reserves. The climbing and steep descents which had to be covered were by any standard treacherous but given our physical condition seemed a challenge too far.

We had no option but to keep going however slow our progress if we wished to survive and so we did, facing impossible odds but always being encouraged by the unfailing will of my dear Mother that we survive to reach my father who was waiting for us.

At about this time we had reached the remnants of a small village in this mountain range, and to our great joy discovered that two Army Personnel had just arrived here from Assam to set up a sort of outpost to help any remnants of survivors over the last stages. They were horrified at our physical condition but pleased to see us in comparatively hopeful spirits having seen other survivors in such poor mental and physical condition. They told us that the Military Authorities were aware of the possibility of there being a few survivors from the Trek through the Hukawng Valley still trying to reach the Border

One of these Military men was one 'Denis Rosner'. He had, at a later stage, been put in charge of Kachin Troops who, under his Command, defeated an attack by the Japanese in the Kachin hills. This Army Officer was later to be appointed as Commanding Officer covering the area between Sumprabum and the Naga Hills i.e. the territory through which we had Trekked all these months! Learning of this we now knew that Japanese forces had in fact advanced north of Myitkyina and into the Kachin Hills. It seemed that the choice we made at Sumprabum was in the end one of two evils and the wisdom of this choice will forever remain unknown!

These men were established in the only hut available and we were to spend the night under the shelter of our makeshift tent. Nevertheless we were overjoyed at the thought of meeting civilised people and of obtaining some medical needs and tinned rations from them. They were also able to give us vital information concerning the nature of the land from here on. We were pleased to know that we were nearing our goal and that the Authorities were aware of our possible survival. They confirmed that as far as they were aware, we were the last group of survivors who had come through the Hell of Shingbwiyang.

All this sounded wonderful to our ears and we had reason to be hopeful were it not for the fact that by now my brother Victor was desperately ill, raving in the delirium of a high fever. The only medicine available from the military men were quinine and aspirins and these we administered to him frequently. Seeing him in this state, when it seemed that our goal was in sight, broke out hearts which would otherwise have been relishing the near success of our impossible venture. The thought of losing him was too sad a prospect to accept.

Whilst at this post we were surprised to find that in one of the small huts, sitting in a dazed state, was a white woman. To all appearances dead - with eyes fixed in an unnatural stare. We were shocked to realise that she was in fact just about alive. She registered pleasure at seeing us by a feeble attempt at a smile. Her skin hung so loosely on the bones of her face that every movement must have been painful to her. I well remember holding her frail hand gently and wiping her face with a piece of cloth dipped in rain water. I felt I was acting as my dear Mother would have done! Her example and courage permeated so much of my mind! We later heard that this woman had been given help and so survived. From her we were to have confirmation of the fate of our family who embarked on the same route as she did and whose remains we had encountered earlier.

Her survival was nothing short of a miracle. She had been amongst those who had set out previous to the rivers becoming impassable and had seen all her family die on the way, with thousands of others.

We left this outpost an even sadder little band, for my brother Victor was now being carried by Naga bearers on a bamboo stretcher. About a week's Trek from here we were met by a British Army Major - a man of robust physical stature. This Major, whilst meaning to prove of the utmost help, had no idea of what we had been through or of the poor state of our bodily reserves, evident though this must have been!

After meeting him we had to cover a patch of jungle, covered in needle like cones which were agony to our bare feet. I can remember this Major attempting to spare Patsy and me this suffering by picking us up by our bony arms. Little did he know that the pain he was inflicting on our arms and shoulders was far worse than the torture of walking on those cones! In addition, at the end of a day's march, he suggested that we attempt physical exercises of the 'keep fit' nature but whereas we were grateful for any help, we were by no means beyond proving our unwillingness to co-operate in his well-meaning 'charades'. How could he have known what we had endured to get here!

CHAPTER TWENTY SEVEN

"The last Lap"

We were now in the second week of November, very near the border by this time and whereas we should have been feeling relieved at having nearly reached our goal we were denied this because of our deep concern over my Brother Victor's condition. We were urged to continue on our own with the promise of my brother following but we refused and they eventually made arrangements for him to accompany us on a stretcher, carried by Naga bearers. We were now descending steep hills and the path we followed skirted the hills, for the most part. We chose each step with the utmost care, not willing to break our necks at the winning post - so to speak! The descent of these hills was perilous and we were often physically unable to control our limbs during this stage. I remember falling badly and were it not for Gloria's strength in grabbing me I might not have survived the steep fall.

It was on this last lap that, in negotiating a particularly steep incline, the Nagas had lost their footing and dropped the stretcher on which my brother was being carried. In addition to his high fever, he was now suffering severe back injuries. Our few paltry belongings which we had fixed to his stretcher landed in the Ravine below - his precious diary being part of it. We were just thankful that they had not lost him to the Ravine as well.

This incident filled us with an unimaginable sadness. To us it seemed that if Victor was not to survive, what right had we. Amidst our tears, we recalled my Mother's faith and courage during the many crises we had endured and so we prayed again. My brother Victor was such a wholly wonderful human being, always thinking of others and he, more than any of us, at the time, shared my Mother's Faith in equal measure. To see him lying there so ill was to us the summit of our endurance.

We continued descending the lower hill which seemed to end in a succession of narrow steps which were carved out of the hill and edged with logs. Apparently these were the celebrated 'Golden Stairs'. Although encouraged by their existence we were very wary of tackling them with any speed given our condition.

We realized just what a danger they would be in Monsoon conditions. I cannot recall the exact number of Steps. There were many. On this dry day they were a sort of return to 'normality' bearing in mind the tortuous nature of so many descents during the Trek.

Once we had reached flat land, we found that a narrow road was being made. We stopped short, at the distant sound of an automobile engine, not believing our ears, and then to our great joy, saw first one Jeep and then another approaching.

Words fail me in describing our feelings at that moment - it just seemed too much to believe after all those months of suffering and hoping. These Jeeps belonged to an American outpost stationed at Ledo on the border of India and they had been told that refugees were expected to come through at any time so they had set out to spare us the last mile or two of trekking! The momentous date forever etched on my memory was **15**th **November 1942.**

The Americans were also shocked at our physical condition but amazed at our spirits. They treated us like heroes and could not do enough to make up for our noticeable lack of material comforts. They put all their rations at our disposal but sorely tempted though we were at the sight of all the food they offered, we were closely watched by our Army friend. He had warned us that, to indulge at this stage, could have proved disastrous to our weakened stomachs. They also provided us with some medicinal needs which we so appreciated. After expressing our gratitude and posing with them, for what must be the only record on print of our condition on arrival, we were taken by rail-car to the Indian army base of Margherita, not far down the line. My Brother was taken with us on a stretcher, still in a high fever.

On arrival here we were ushered to allotted army tents since this was purely a Military area, and we were told that we would remain here for a few days till arrangements could be made for our departure to an appropriate reception centre. Victor was housed in the Military Hospital Tent, under the care of Army Medical Staff. Here we were to be given food and nourishment, appropriate to our needs at the time.

It was on the second day of our stay at this camp that we were to experience a final threat to our survival. The wailing of sirens, amidst army orders being shouted in all directions, told us that we were to flee for the shelter of any available ditch. Once more it seemed, Japanese aircraft were intent on depositing their bombs in the vicinity of our abode! Having survived so much, the irony of the situation seemed bizarre were it not so threatening. Although we spent most of that day sheltering under a bridge, whilst the air was filled with Anti-aircraft fire from the guns positioned all around us, we seemed strangely indifferent to the danger. It was only the safety of my brother who was in the hospital tent that concerned us.

We remained in our semi-sheltered position till dusk when the all clear sounded. We were then able to check on Victor's condition which was very serious. Although he was receiving all available medical attention we hated having to be separated from him but we had no option. We returned to our tent, sad, weary and longing to lie down on our camp beds - a luxury at this stage, which we were unable to appreciate because of our anxiety. The Military officials were now concerned that we be moved out as soon as possible.

By contact with the Authorities at the Digboi Oil Refinery (an associate Company of the Burmah Oil company for which my father worked) where our plight had become known, my brother was removed to the Hospital at Digboi a few miles from Margherita. We ourselves were allowed to accompany him and be handed over to the care of a close family friend who was at this time stationed here. The two girls in our charge were taken over by the authorities at Marghreta to be moved to the Hospital in the area, where refugees were being cared for.

Victor - my much loved Brother in healthier and happier times

When recalling this period I remember how unreal it all seemed and the vacuum we felt within our hearts. Somehow it did not yet register that we had reached our goal because we had hoped to succeed as a family group and we were now so few - just us five girls. The fact that we had not yet reached my Father may well have reflected in our feelings at this stage and there was also the heartbreaking situation of Victor being so ill.

CHAPTER TWENTY EIGHT

"A Final Heartbreak"

Within a day of our arrival at Digboi we were called to the deathbed of my Brother. His sad death was in many ways harder to bear than previous tragedies because, now in near normal surroundings, we had become so much more vulnerable to the sadness of our loss. Having gone through so much together and being so near to having successfully survived, made his death all the more tragic in our eyes. The only small comfort we had was that he, at least, was afforded the kind of burial we had wished possible for those loved ones whom we had lost on that perilous Trek.

The Assam Oil Company very kindly made arrangements for my Brother's funeral which we girls attended, with kind friends and many people who had been so moved by our experience that they were there to support us. We were strangely unconcerned as to our physical appearance suffice to say that we had been given clothing and personal necessities by the kind people at the Reception Post in Margherita. We had long since accepted our frail appearance in the reality of our achievement. All I remember of this day was suffering the desperate loss of someone so loving and caring and whom we loved so much but I also knew that his last days were a trial he did not deserve. I felt strongly that my Mother was there to welcome him!

Our saddened hearts were somewhat uplifted by the news that my brother Frank and his companion had survived and that he had reached Calcutta. They had apparently trekked those last 150 odd miles over the Patkoi Mountain Range in just over two weeks, which was in his condition a super human effort. He has mentioned nothing of the horrors of that journey. However, we know that to have done it unaided in that time, with so few provisions, and bearing in mind his physical condition, must have taken immense courage and determination. We took this to be yet another miracle. Frank refused to speak of the Trek until the last few years of his life, following severe strokes, when he did speak to me about it. His faith had returned and he seemed more at ease talking about the past, including the Trek.

Though his efforts had not accomplished the mission he had in mind when setting out from Shingbwiyang i.e. to get help in time to save my Mother, his safe arrival had made his brave efforts well worthwhile.

CHAPTER TWENTY NINE

"Reaching my Father at last"

Whilst we were at Digboi we learned that my Father had been anxiously awaiting news of us all those months following up every hearsay of our possible whereabouts and fate. He obtained employment in this area just so that he be within easy reach of the border. As a matter of fact, he had only left Digboi a few days previous to our arrival, having been advised by the Military Authorities to go to Gauhati. This was where the refugees were to be sent on reaching the border. Were it not for the fact that we had been given special permission to accompany my brother to Digboi we would have gone straight to Gauhati where my Father was waiting for us.

So it was that my Father learned the sad news concerning my Mother and Victor and for the first time knew that the rest of us girls had survived. As the train pulled into the station, at Gauhati, we could see him anxiously looking out for us no doubt expecting us to be carried on stretchers, whereas, we barely waited for the train to halt, before I rushed over to where he stood, the others following. So many tears were shed but just being able to hug us to him gave him the strength to appreciate this moment. Our physical condition must have been a shock to him but to find us in such good spirits gave him the assurance he needed as to our having survived. I remember thinking how thin my dear Dad looked and later came to know how much he had suffered knowing of our plight. I could not begin to express our emotions at this meeting - seeing my Father at last! Suffice that I say this was the moment for which we had endured so much, defied death and fought so hard against impossible odds. We were now fulfilling my beloved Mother's greatest wish and there are truly no words to describe our feelings at this momentous time.

CHAPTER THIRTY

"The Follow Through"

Although this is essentially the story of my Trek out of Burma I feel sure the reader would wish to know a little of what followed this unforgettable experience and so I take the liberty of adding a brief synopsis of the immediate 'follow through' of my life.

On being reunited with my Father we were taken to Calcutta following a 'de-briefing' as it were by the Military Authorities in Gauhati. Here we were subjected to questioning of a bizarre nature considering the experience we had just endured. These Authorities would however, not have known anything of our experience and were bent on carrying out safeguard checks concerning possible Japanese Spy infiltration, as instructed to do! At one point the questioning and physical examinations we were subjected to so angered my Sister Joyce, that she screamed her objection to the Military Authorities! My Father immediately called for help from the Oil Company personnel at Digboi to obtain our immediate release from this Camp in our fragile state. We were then permitted to leave with my Father for Calcutta where my Mother's youngest brother and my brother Frank awaited our arrival.

This was a highly emotional reunion for so many reasons. Firstly, it was the final confirmation that we had made it and it was a very moving experience for us. We were being re-united with my Brother Frank whom we had not expected to ever see again, given the impossible task he had undertaken and our situation when he left us. There was much hugging, crying and laughter too of which we had enjoyed so little since leaving our home. We realised at this point that our systems were absorbing quite a shock in being exposed to the extreme noise of a busy city like Calcutta after being 'lost' in the jungles all these months!

Our emotions were very mixed and we found it hard to take in the 'normality' of our surroundings but Patsy and I just held on to my Father's hands and felt secure at last. We must have looked so 'strange' being skeletal, with hardly any hair on our heads and wearing 'soft shoes' which we had been supplied with at Gauhati. This was all we could bear on our very sore feet at this time. Our will and spirits far outstripped our physical condition as we made our way to my Uncle's home in Calcutta. Gloria's Sister and family were there to meet her and she left us with many emotional hugs being exchanged. We did of course, keep in close touch in the years following.

We were overjoyed to be welcomed in my Uncle's home and within a few days were settled in the Flat next door. My Sister Phyllis was admitted to a hospital in Calcutta for observation and all of us were brought under the care of my Uncle's Doctor. There was much repair needed!

We were now nearing Christmas 1942 and we had barely enjoyed more than a week's re-settlement when Sirens sounded sending chills down our spines. My Father and Uncle hurriedly ushered us to the Basement of the building in which we were living. Very soon we heard the familiar drone of Aircraft accompanied by Anti-aircraft fire from the gun positions surrounding us and then the familiar pounding of Japanese Bombs in our vicinity. Houses behind us were subject to direct hits, fires burning everywhere and the screams of the occupants left us shaken, reliving so much of our past horror. We spent a good few days and nights running for the shelter of this Basement and this made my Father decide that we must leave Calcutta immediately. My Father collected my Sister Phyllis from the Hospital and decided that he would immediately evacuate us to the safety of Belgaum - a small British Military Cantonment in South West India. We set out on a 3-day Rail journey across India to reach Belgaum. It was here that the family of Sid Hearsey our close friend, who housed us when we first arrived at Digboi, were now safely settled.

We owe much to the loving care of the dear Hearsey family in helping to restore us to reasonable health. We were given good food, much nourishment and an abundance of love and nursing, all of which we needed badly and so it was that our bodies responded and our medical condition was much improved. However, we continued to suffer severe Malaria attacks and I was troubled with the Dysentery germ for many months to come. The Doctor at Belgaum took us under his wing being very moved by our achievement and condition. He gave us the best Treatment available and we remained indebted to him for his care and help.

Here in this peaceful little town, in the home of this loving family, we were given the opportunity to recoup a little and gain strength to accept the challenge of picking up the threads of our lives again. My Father had left us here knowing that we would be safe and well looked after, since he had to return to the War Zone in Assam to take up employment again with the Assam Oil Company.

Here am I - 9 months after the Trek.
Hair re-grown and looking fairly normal on the outside!
It took much longer for our hearts and minds to heal.

We stayed at Belgaum for the next five months and returned to Calcutta in May of 1943. My Sister Joyce, married her fiancé George who was now a serving member of the Calcutta Police. He had been with my Father in the Demolition of the Refinery at Syriam. My Sister Phyllis went to live with an Aunt and Uncle who were now settled in the suburbs of Calcutta. My brother Frank joined my Father in Assam to work with him. Patsy and myself were sent to School as Boarders later in the year, as Calcutta was thought to be in the danger zone at this time for many reasons. We were not allowed to join my Father who was working in a prohibited Military area in Assam at the time.

This was a very difficult time for Patsy and myself but having each other helped us survive. We were later moved to a Convent Hill-School in Assam which was nearer my Father, where we completed our senior education and where the Nuns looked after us well. Here we were as happy as we could be given our circumstances and were later allowed to go home to my Father for holidays which so pleased us. We owe much to these dear Nuns who, knowing of our experience, treated us very kindly besides giving us the benefit of a good education, which saw us qualified to Senior Matriculation standard within a comparatively short time.

The history of the recapture of Burma bears witness to the expertise, courage and fortitude of so many brave Soldiers on many fronts of this Campaign. It was a horrendous War in which the nature of the Country made warfare even more treacherous. Many books have been written on this subject and all of them bear testimony to these facts. However, Burma was recaptured and we were to now wonder whether it could be home to us again!

My Father was then transferred to Burma to work at the Refinery at Syriam in September of 1947and so we returned. My sister Joyce and her family had arrived in Burma a few months earlier. My Sister Phyllis met her husband-to-be whilst we were in India and left us early in 1948 to be married there. We hated parting with her but were reunited years later to enjoy many happy times with her and her family here in England.

We soon found that returning to Burma was not a good idea. Our home had been ruined during the war and was now compulsorily occupied by natives of the country. We found it heartbreaking to walk the familiar streets again and soon realised that we had made a big mistake in returning, given the circumstances. We could not help but return, in our minds and hearts, to the days where my Story began and being here again after all that happened made it unreal and beyond coping with. So within the year, my Father, Frank, Patsy and myself set sail for England in September 1948 leaving a Country which we had so loved and enjoyed living in before the War. The many political changes which had ensued meant that we were no longer welcome in the Country and it was no longer home to us. Joyce and family followed us to Reigate in the County of Surrey, the following year.

We sailed into Tilbury Docks on a very cold, foggy November morning which did not exactly provide a warm welcome for us! We made our way to Victoria station where we were met by the Hearsey family who had so lovingly taken us to their hearts and home in Belgaum. They were now living in Reigate where we started our lives in England back in 1948. We have always felt this to have been a good move in securing happy futures for us all.

The Closure with Acknowledgements

My story ends here, though there was much to remind us of our ordeal in the years to come. All that we had endured had most certainly put our Faith to trial but there were also so many miracles to strengthen it. Several thousands had embarked on this Trek with the same purpose in mind so why should we have, if not by God's will, be among the very few who survived. Our closeness as a family had, no doubt, been instrumental in giving us the common bond with which to fight such impossible odds. The immense faith and courage of my dear Mother was our never failing hope of survival.

Through the years that followed we each made happy lives of our own remaining a very close family and always so pleased to be together. However, never having made a conscious decision to not refer to this horrendous experience, it seems that none of us wished its recall to invade our lives again!

So much of it was too painful to reflect on and I think each of us was reluctant to 'Open the Lid' to our memories of that tortuous Trek. It is also true to say that we did not wish my dear Father to know exactly what we had been through nor the details concerning my beloved Mother's suffering and death. I also feel my Father was fearful of the effect it may have had on us to discuss our experience and we in turn so wanted to protect him from the truth. For all these reasons, we chose to leave the memories of this period of our lives unspoken, though each of us carried our own 'image' of what it meant to us. I alone had always wished to record our experience and did attempt to do this twenty-five years later, when living in Canada. However the same emotional restrictions existed as set out above, so I have not felt free until now to delve further and finally achieve my aim.

In writing my story I am amazed at the permanence of detail stored in my memory concerning the Trek. I remember so much of the exact positions of people, places and things. Names have been 'filed' in an unbelievable way. How could it be that my very young mind absorbed and held all of this, through so many years, without fading into at least part confusion!

It can only be because the impact of it was so profound as to preserve all the detail in my heart and mind. I remain indebted to my beloved Mother for inheriting her courage and strength to never allow our experience to rob me of my will to make the most of our survival!

Sadly, I lost my dear Father in 1974. My Sister Joyce died suddenly in 1985. Patsy tragically died of Motor Neurone Disease in 1995 and Frank died in 1997 following several Strokes. Neither of them had children. My sister Phyllis died in 2008 aged 88. My Sister Joyce's husband George died in 2005 aged 87. Gloria moved away to Australia where she settled happily with her family. We eventually lost touch with her after many years.

Today, I am the lone survivor of our family and it is for the benefit of our children and grandchildren and the families of my sisters Joyce and Phyllis that I have recalled this tortuous experience in depth. I hope that in the reading of my 'Trek Story' our family will find courage in dealing with difficult times and also, perhaps, strengthen their faith in God.

Many years have passed since this episode in my life and whilst I have found good reason to write my Story I know that I would not have 'survived' the attempt, were it not for the security of my own long, happy, marriage and loving family. We have been blessed with a Daughter and Son and three lovely Granddaughters all of whom are so close to our hearts. Above all I owe my dearest husband Gerry my heartfelt gratitude for all the help he has given me in producing my script, using all of his 'Computer skills' and displaying a lot of patience with my constant need to insert yet another 'memory flash'. His loving encouragement has enabled me to endure the strain of re-visiting all of this very painful experience in my life..........